FAMILIES

Celebration and hope in a world of change

FAMILIES

Celebration and hope in a world of change

Jo Boyden

Published in co-operation with UNESCO

Gaia Books Limited

A GAIA ORIGINAL

Written by Jo Boyden
with additional material by
Maggie Black and Wendy Davies

Project Editor	Philip Parker
Design	Lucy Guenot
Production Editor	Michelle Atkinson
Illustration	Aziz Khan
	Ann Savage
Picture Research	Elly Beintema
Production	Susan Walby
Direction	Joss Pearson
	Patrick Nugent
UNESCO Consultants	Robert Myers
	John Bennett

This is a Registered Trade Mark
of Gaia Books Limited

First published in the United Kingdom in 1993 by
Gaia Books Limited
66 Charlotte Street   and   20 High Street
London W1P 1LR   Stroud, Glos GL5 1AS

Typeset by Spectrum, London
Printed by Craft Print, Singapore

A catalogue record of this book is available from the British Library

ISBN 1 85675 041 8

10 9 8 7 6 5 4 3 2 1

Families all over the world are as different as they are alike. Some live in love, others live in fear. Some live together, others are separated or dispersed in distant places where they have been forcibly brought by war, ethnic strife, poverty, and the search for bread for their kin.

The International Year of the Family, which this valuable publication commemorates, has been proclaimed by the General Assembly of the United Nations to raise the world's awareness of the plight of families, and for the existence, harmony, and wellbeing of their individual members. The purposes and objectives of the Year are concerned with families' responsibilities as much as they are with their rights. Its sparkling epigram, "Building the smallest democracy at the heart of society", indicates an ideal objective of our efforts during and after the Year.

Does this mean that the International Year of the Family will aim to establish one "positive" or "ideal" definition or form of the family? Not at all. The unity that the Year seeks on family issues is one of diversity. The concept of pluralism defines present-day human relations. The world's societies form its richest reflection; their basic units are families.

To strengthen families the first major consideration is to offer equal chances to all the individuals comprising them. In the pursuit of such an objective, adherence to internationally agreed human rights and social policy standards is of paramount importance. These include the provisions of the International Covenant on Economic, Social and Cultural Rights, the UN Convention on the Elimination of All Forms of Discrimination Against Women, and the UN Convention on the Rights of the Child.

It is in the spirit of a pluralistic search for common denominators, shared approaches, and unifying elements regarding family issues that the Secretariat for the International Year of the Family has been supporting initiatives and ventures that contribute to achieving the objectives of the Year, including this book. It is hoped they will make a valuable contribution to a challenging discourse on the world's families that is at the heart of the International Year of the Family.

Henryk J. Sokalski
Co-ordinator for the International Year of the Family

the international year of the family

International Year of the Family 1994

Family life is most precious. It is the natural environment for the growth and wellbeing of all family members, particularly children. Mutual respect, gender equality, solid inter-generational links, and supportive emotional bonding should be its hallmarks.

The wish of groups and couples to create stable environments for themselves and their children runs strong and deep. Present difficulties encountered in family life are often a reflection of far-reaching economic, social, and demographic changes. The end of the century continues to be marked by such changes – and, with them, by family dysfunction and breakdown. Yet there are also some important signs of hope. There is today, for example, a more just understanding of the ill effects of poverty on the family. Governments and non-governmental organizations are making enormous strides in providing basic welfare – clean water, shelter, basic health, nutrition, and education – to their populations. Likewise, countries are introducing – and trying to make effective – legislation, policies, and support services as they realize that social and family cohesion is conducive to development.

During certain critical years, almost all parents need support in their task of providing care and education for their children. Even more so, vulnerable families – single-parent families, families without shelter or income, immigrant families, destabilized families, or families with special needs – need the support of the extended family, the community, and society at large.

The aim of social support is not to take away parental functions or to make families the passive recipients of social care. Having children creates responsibility and will normally motivate parents to carry out their biological, psychological, economic, and educational functions: to impart care and protection; offer love and healthy family relationships; provide shelter and material welfare; and promote play and learning.

Societies will do well, however, to support responsible attitudes to parenthood by educating adolescents and young adults in parenting skills and providing support systems for parents in their child-rearing tasks.

The International Year of the Family in 1994 provides the occasion for reflection on the family as the "smallest democracy at the heart of society". In this connection it is well to recall that for democracies to live, they must learn to change. At the end of our century a decisive change that the family must bring about within its own confines is the equality of men and women, both in their rights and responsibilities.

The family can no longer be used as an alibi for the social or educational downgrading of women and girls. Freedom to earn and learn is the right of all individuals. Societies have a duty to allow this right to be enjoyed by women. At the same time, parenting must be revalued and enhanced. There is no more vital social role than the care and education of children. The decisive role of the mother, particularly with regard to young children, is recognized, if not always rewarded. By contrast, expectations concerning the father are frequently weak.

The phenomenon of the absent father is widespread. His reduced participation in parenting is sometimes the result of external causes such as migration for work, but more often, it is the result of deep-seated cultural attitudes and gender stereotyping. Even in what should be fairly ideal circumstances, fathers often spend little time with their children. Yet, the research suggests that many mothers are, as a result, overworked, and that boys, in particular, suffer from paternal absence. In addition, non-support by fathers undermines the economic base of a growing number of women-headed families.

UNESCO's work for the International Year of the Family has been along three main lines: translating the general objectives of the Year into practical educational and cultural goals; placing the family on the international research agenda, in particular its educational and cultural functions; and raising public awareness of the fundamental role of the family in the education of children.

I congratulate Jo Boyden and Gaia Books on creating this thought-provoking book for the International Year of the Family. I trust that its publication will promote the cause of education and lead to useful reflection and action.

Federico Mayor
Director General of UNESCO

introduction by Peter Ustinov

At the basis of all life is the inescapable fact that every human being is alone on this Earth, imprisoned for better or for worse in a body not of its inhabitant's choosing. Sometimes this essential solitude is a blessing, at other moments it can be a reason to panic. This part of the human condition would be too cruel if there were not a variety of rich consolations which can only exist because people are isolated from one another. There is, of course, love, the rarest of balms, which in its purest and most successful forms, renders a person oblivious to his or her aloneness, at least for long stretches at a time. On an only slightly less elevated level there is friendship, a human warmth less exhausting and therefore easier to maintain than love. And then there is a cut-price compromise called companionship, which is making the best of what's at hand, without getting unduly concerned about compatibility or mutual interest.

There is also the family, which is ideally the creation of two people in love, becoming eventually the most desirable yet most complicated of all tests of character on this Earth. There are many pitfalls inherent in the family unit, one of the most dangerous being that children become the victims of their parents' unreasonable hopes. How many sons in the past have fallen prey to their fathers' insistence that footsteps be followed, and how many possessive mothers have outstayed their welcome by occupying all their sons' attentions far too late in life? And how many daughters have been pursued throughout their youth by

The family: the fundamental building block of societies everywhere (left).

an unexpressed regret that they were not boys, and were therefore confined to functions which past generations thought fit for women?

And sometimes, whether the family fails or not, there are collectives preferred by certain temperaments; the armed forces, convents, monasteries, clubs, secret societies, gangs, the Mafia. Ironically, they even refer to the Mafia as *La Familia*, suggesting that blood ties do not have to be natural, but can even be forged by mutual interests. But whatever the value of interest attached to some of these artificial agglomerations of people, nothing is half as fascinating as the family imagined by a couple and brought to a reality sometimes totally different from their individual hopes. One of the drawbacks of an increasingly technological existence is that it has caused, especially in advanced societies, a deadening of the instinct, and a self-consciousness about the facts of life and of living.

Religious leaders and politicians tend to idealize the family unit, maintaining that it is the vital element in the structure of society. It would be foolish and indeed pretentious to allege that they are wrong, merely to suggest that there are occasions in which a broken family exposed to the evident risk of disintegration is preferable to a united family, festering in its own claustrophobia. When the ideals are talked about, there is never any admission of the possible development of madness in a member of the family, or even destructive developments commensurate with temporary insanity such as addiction to alcohol and drugs, or wife or husband beating, under which observant children suffer even more in the long term than those engaged in such indulgences.

What is more heartbreaking than to see a family destroyed in a war zone? Where both parents are dead, or have disappeared, and in which a child, smoking from a cupped hand and speaking with rough objectivity in a voice prematurely grave, has assumed the leadership of his little clan, a leadership accepted by his younger brothers and sisters. This shows as

A single parent with a child (right) is the smallest family form. Lone parenthood is a growing phenomenon in both the industrialized and developing worlds.

nothing else the extraordinary resilience of the family under tragic conditions, and equally of its practically unbreakable ties.

God knows, there are enough unpredictable strains on a perfectly normal family, with rational parents and healthy children, to make its survival at times speculative. Misfortune has a tendency to harden the resolve to survive by opening hearts and minds to problems linking all mankind. Sharing is one of the greatest comforts and imparters of wisdom in existence. It is learned in the family for general application elsewhere.

Children learn by watching, and the gift of observation is often merciless toward unscrupulous or negligent parents, who may well be pious in what they preach yet careless in their practices. A sometimes painful yet essential moment in development is the discovery that parents are human, and even if children are children for the first and only time, they sometimes fail to realize (how could they?) that parents are as inexperienced in their roles as children are in theirs. I have said, and I believe it more and more, that one function of parents too rarely talked about is that they are the bones on which the puppies sharpen their teeth. This can be somewhat painful, yet it is absolutely vital.

Mothers carry a child for nine months of increasing discomfort, whereas fathers look on with evident pride in their achievement, and advance chains for mother and unborn child. This ritual ends immediately the child is born. Amid moments of concern and mutual consideration, the father's sleep, so vital for his work, is interrupted by screaming, while mother seems to become more and more attached to her baby's problems, sometimes at

Families not only raise children, live and
eat together, and share sadness and joy –
many also work together, whether farming
or fishing (above).

the expense of her husband's. As the family grows, unplumbed elements of humility and understanding must be found to assist in the parents' process of learning the functions of parenthood. It is quite normal, and indeed rather touching, that mothers and fathers should see in their childrens' physical features and actions, reflections of their own personalities and looks. And yet it is important to admit from the outset that, whereas babies are the creation of two people, they are themselves third parties, independent even if indebted, isolated even if protected. They are an extension of that necessary human solitude from the moment of their birth, and the victory of the family is to make this possible.

Like everything else in nature, the family is subject to continuous change. That which is static in nature, dies. Children grow up, parents grow old, other children are born. We know about the endless cycle of life, and it is the glory of the family that it is the logical team to make the best and face the worst of what this world has to offer. It is a practical example of the necessary interdependence of the human race, able, ideally, to counter most vicissitudes and even to accept generalizations and platitudes with that necessary pinch of salt.

In hunter-gatherer as well as industrial societies, the nuclear, two-generation family predominates. This family (left) belongs to an indigenous group in the Philippines.

Families today face a number of social and economic pressures. Many Brazilian families, for instance, experience poverty and landlessness (below), but they may draw strength from their unity.

prologue

"Far from being the basis of the good society, the family with its narrow privacy and tawdry secrets, is the source of all our discontents."
Sir Edmund Leach (Reith Lecture, 1968)

"...When we are considering society from any other point of view than the economic, we can all see well enough that, of all its institutions, the family is after all the institution that matters most. It is at once indispensable as a means to all the rest and, in a sense, an end in itself...the strongest emotions, the most enduring motives, the most universally accessible sources of happiness are concerned with this business of the family."
Eleanor Rathbone (1924)

"Loyalty to the family ranks highest of all, higher even than loyalty to the state. It is no accident...that dictatorships, whether of the Left or the Right, seek first to devalue and then to destroy the family."
Lord Jenkin (1977)

This book is a portrait – in words, photographs, and maps – of the conditions and concerns experienced by families across the world at the turn of the twentieth century.

The scope of the subject is huge. There is an enormous spectrum of cultures, family forms, and interests involved; a turbulent flood of social change, new ideas, and differing expectations. The book celebrates this vibrant diversity, matching global statistics with individual life stories from East to West, rich to poor, city to village.

But there are common threads too, universal in their implications. The book explores the roles, forms, and relationships within families, the challenges they face, and their hopes and needs for the future.

Families bear the brunt of humanity's troubles. At their best, they make a profound contribution to the health of society and its individuals: preserving culture, values, ethics, and wealth; defending the weak; carrying out the great unpaid work of the world. At their worst, they resist change, restrict individual freedom, and indulge in prejudices that can lead to conflict. Their power to form and reshape human minds is forever being rediscovered. Good or ill, we cannot do without them – they are the building blocks of our world. And they are under great pressures today.

The old enemies of the family – poverty, war, and disease – far from abating, are still striking families at their roots. And in a world of rapid change, families too must change. Modern culture with its quest for individualism, largely Western in origin, is spreading to create new, global social norms which upturn older values. New forms of family are emerging – from single parent to partners of the same sex – and new rights, for women, children, the older generation, are demanded. The spreading global norms are confronted by counter surges of ethnic and religious beliefs, and the family is caught between them. Political changes mean that the balance of responsibility, and economic load, between families and the state is shifting. This book explores the consequences of such large changes. Will the family as we have known it survive?

With increasing life expectancy, it is common to find four generations living under one roof, as with this Muslim family in Turkmenistan (above).

the many roles of the family

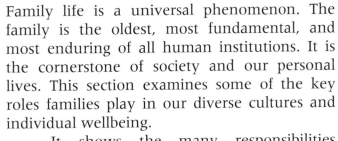

Family life is a universal phenomenon. The family is the oldest, most fundamental, and most enduring of all human institutions. It is the cornerstone of society and our personal lives. This section examines some of the key roles families play in our diverse cultures and individual wellbeing.

It shows the many responsibilities families carry for the wider society. They are the source of the new generation, of population growth or control, and of primary child care. They meet the basic human needs of food and shelter, care for elderly and disabled people, create wealth, and provide large, unrecognized, economic services.

And it explores what the family means to us as individuals. Socializer, educator, and transmitter of culture, tradition, and skills, the family can profoundly influence our human potential and happiness by the care it offers during our youth. All our lives, we turn to it for love and shared values, for support in good times or bad, and for the reference point that gives meaning to our experience.

These roles are challenged by contemporary society. The family is resilient, flexible, a survivor. It could probably flourish (and has certainly shown in the past that it can) without the wider society. But if we erode the role of the family, can the wider society flourish?

Birth: a cause for celebration for the Tuwin herdspeople of Siberia (left) – as it is for peoples the world over. The creation and nurture of children is a central role of families.

Mantras and mothers

Ritual is a vital element in Tibetan childbirth. Tibetans pass their heritage to their children genetically, culturally, and spiritually. Ritual is present at every stage of the birth process, from before conception to early childhood. A woman who wants to have a baby, for example, will go to a holy place to pray. During pregnancy Tibetan women are seen as having access to high spiritual realms. As soon as the infant's mouth is opened, a symbol of wisdom is painted in saffron powder on the newborn's tongue.

• Every day, 910,000 new lives are conceived (WHO).

• About half of all conceptions are unplanned (WHO).

• Leonita Albina, a 65-year-old Chilean woman, is reputedly the "mother of all others" with 55 documented births. She claims to be the mother of 64 children (Guinness Book of Records).

The child – a symbol of life and family continuity – is the focus of attention everywhere. This is particularly true in China (right), where official policy allows only one child per family.

Creating the future

The creation of a new life is always a moment of hope for parents and society alike. The parents have a dream for the child they bring into the world – a vision of the future. Not only is a new person created and given an identity, the parents themselves discover new identities as "mother" and "father".

On Mother's Day in 1990, the French President François Mitterrand received a small group of women at the Elysée Palace. Each of the women had borne eight or more children, and their motherhood was celebrated with the awarding of medals. In France, where increasing the population is a national aim, Mother's Day has become an important political occasion. In any society, new members are required to replace those that have died; otherwise it is doomed to extinction. Everywhere, this task of replacement is given to the family.

Producing new members of a society or a family entails more than the act of procreation. Young human beings are dependent for far longer than any other species. Physical maturation is slow, and the new member takes a long time to learn the complexities of society. Humans have few ready-made instincts at birth. Instead, we have an enormous capacity for learning, and much of what we learn comes from the family.

The tragedy for so many families is that there is no guarantee that their young will survive, be healthy, or develop normally. In Africa, for every 1000 live births, between 150 and 250 children will die before their fifth birthday. Globally, today and every day, 35,000 children under five years of age die. Most of these deaths occur in developing countries from malnutrition and easily preventable diseases spread by poverty.

High child mortality influences parents' views on how many children they want. Only by having a lot of children can parents make sure that enough will survive into adulthood to provide family continuity and support in their old age. Before they contemplate having smaller families, parents need to be confident that their children will live. In wealthy countries, where mortality has fallen dramatically over this century, small families are now more common than large.

In societies where births are plentiful and chances of survival poor, the emotional investment in the newborn may be less than where birth is a novelty and mortality low. In Brazilian shanty towns families wait until the infant is one year old, and they are sure it will thrive, before celebrating its arrival. Only then do they name the baby. By contrast, births in the West are celebrated by "wetting the baby's head", and family and friends give gifts and cards of congratulation. A host of professionals – health visitors, doctors, social workers, nursery staff – are often on hand during the child's first years to assist the parents.

In human society, by tradition, a special bond exists between a child's parents. In most cases they are long-term sexual partners who share their lives and concerns. Marriage provides for the formal, contractual organization of family life. But there is no inevitable link between family and children; many children are raised in alternative environments, such as orphanages, and births take place and children reared outside marriage.

New cultural patterns are rapidly emerging in the industrialized world, profoundly affecting the relationship between marriage, sex, and reproduction. Changes in women's status, and the availability of contraception and other reproductive technologies, mean that sexuality and reproduction are increasingly separated. Families are now forming around a relationship

the life-giver

For most of us, the family is the principal influence on our behaviour. It is where we learn how to behave and how to live in society. These three-year-olds are preparing for adult life through their play (left).

of choice rather than through a duty to Nature to reproduce. Parenthood outside a formal, marital relationship is commonplace. A half of all births in the UK in 1990, for example, were to unmarried women.

When a baby laughs or frowns, makes a characteristic gesture, or starts to talk, people often remark that the child is the "spitting image" of a parent, or a close family member. This is not simply a case of physical inheritance. Babies copy and learn the mannerisms, expressions, and speech of those around them. As the group we come into most contact with when we are young, the family has a major influence on the way we think and act. From our family we learn the attitudes, behaviours, and ways of living that are appropriate to our cultural and social standing.

We learn from family contact throughout our lives; each important experience, such as marriage, having children, or retiring, brings new patterns of behaviour with it. Learning is most intense during infancy and childhood. The mother is normally the principal teacher of the very young child, at least until weaning. But as the infant's horizons expand, so other people

Home help

The ways in which parents help children's development in the home takes many forms. Three-quarters of parents in a study of 790 families in Nebraska, US, explained that the reason for giving children domestic chores was that it was "character-building". Only 22 parents responded that they needed help in the home.

begin to have growing influence. Older siblings, especially sisters, are important because often they care for the young child. In many cultures grandparents play a vital part. Indeed, extended families can maintain and hand down tradition far more readily than smaller nuclear families, which produce short-lived households that dissolve at the parents' death.

In the family children learn about themselves, and what it means in society to be handicapped or sick, black or white, and boy or girl. In most cultures, the sex of a child largely determines his or her pattern of learning: boys and girls are treated differently and taught very different skills, values, and behaviour. Often, it is adults of the same sex as the child who take on the job of teaching. Children cannot learn in abstract terms: their learning needs to fit their everyday experience. In the West, for example, girls are encouraged to be passive and gentle by playing games that are ordered and quiet. They learn about mothering and wifely roles by playing with dolls. Boys are usually encouraged to be physically active and assertive, to play with construction sets and toy guns. They are allowed to get dirty and explore the world about them.

"From our family we learn our attitudes, behaviours, and ways of living"

There are major differences between cultures in the way children learn. The concept of "childhood" as it is known in industrialized countries today – a period of dependence and innocence – is recent and largely Western. In many other contemporary cultures, children are still thought of as miniature adults. They learn by exposure to adult life rather than being secluded from it in schools or the home. In poor rural communities particularly, children have no guaranteed access to school and little time for play. Production on the rural smallholding relies on traditional techniques passed on by elders within the family. At just four or five years of age children are working alongside their parents or other relatives.

In the West learning is a more conscious and formal process. Education in the school is necessary because the industrial worker needs academic qualifications and technical skills in a rapidly changing society. Many forces intervene in children's learning in industrialized societies. Media influences on child

*"The family has
a key role in the
social placement
of its members"*

development and peer influence during the teenage years are particularly powerful. Increasingly, these forces are seen as threats to family life. The family, some fear, will eventually be deprived of its key function as teacher.

We are all fascinated with our origins – our "roots". Some people travel halfway across the world, at great expense, to trace ancestors and draw up a family tree.

The family exerts a powerful influence over its members, requiring them to respect and preserve the blood line, conserve family tradition and class, and protect the family's reputation. Our ancestry has considerable bearing on our expectations in life. The ability of the family to control destiny stretches across the generations; some believe it stems from the dead. Ancestral cults are important in many societies.

The compelling concept of dynasty is recognized in diverse cultures throughout the world. The glossy American television production, "Dynasty", has proved to be one of the most popular series ever shown internationally. It features many of the potent fantasies of family life – glamour, affluence, and passionate love – and some of its sinister aspects as well – greed, jealousy, violence, and possessiveness.

The family exerts a powerful influence over its members. The caste of millions in India is decided in the womb and persists even into the tomb. Contact with "untouchables" is deemed hazardous, and many live outside society (left).

the dynasty-maker

Some of the world's famous dynasties, such as the Kennedy family in the United States, are founded on wealth and power. Others, the Sicilian Mafia or the Colombian drug cartels, for instance, are founded on crime. Dynastic crime, unfortunately, pays: the Colombian drug barons are reputedly among the wealthiest men in the world. A few dynasties are ennobled by royal blood: the Thai royal family, for instance, is ennobled to such a degree that the king is virtually a god. Dynasties are the stuff of which history is made; larger than life, they confer great benefits on their members, but can be very vulnerable to the misdemeanours of individuals.

The advantages of belonging to an important dynasty contrast with the tyranny of heritage for those born into the class of the underdog. The status and fate of over 100 million dalits – or untouchables – in India is decided in the womb, and cannot be changed even after they are in the tomb. The traditional Indian caste system divides people on the basis of occupation, but denies equal rights and status to different groups. Historically, the dalits were serfs or slaves who served the other castes by doing such menial jobs as latrine cleaning and street sweeping. People are believed to be born dalits because of heinous sins committed in previous lives; physical contact with a dalit is hazardous – hence the concept of "untouchability".

Ancient lineage

The oldest, traceable lineage in Europe is the O'Neill dynasty of Ireland. It is the most famous branch of the ancient royal family of Tara, whose recorded filiation is accepted by scholars from about 360 AD. The O'Neills gave High Kings to all Ireland from the fifth century until the thirteen century and reigned from AD425 until 1603 in Northern Ireland. Their surname was the first to be adopted in Ireland and means "the grandson of Niall". The family was lorded four generations ago and the present Lord O'Neill still resides in Ireland.

Laws have been passed in India for justice and equity for dalits, but for the majority, untouchability remains an everyday reality. It bars millions of people from village wells and Hindu temples, and forces them into virtual slavery. Many dalits seek to hide their ancestry. Others try to escape the caste system by becoming Buddhist converts.

In society, the family has a key role in the "social placement" of its members. Its many virtues are thus balanced by its power to persuade members to conform and by its vigorous hold over people's fate.

The home is central to family life, whatever form it takes. The pavement-dwelling family in Bombay (right) takes great pride in its shelter and garden.

Sustaining the family

The family's daily life and many important events, from birth to death, take place in the home. It is here that family members receive shelter and sustenance. Home is possibly the most important place in all our lives; it is where we belong and feel secure.

In the West, establishing a home absorbs the lion's share of family income. Houses must be built to strict aesthetic and building standards, and home-making has become a massive industry, spawning a bewildering array of occupations, from the bricklayer and plasterer to the real estate agent. Land prices are *the homemaker*

often inflated and property speculation is rife – all adding to the cost of owning or renting a home. In countries where home ownership is common, most families have to borrow considerable sums of money to buy. They may have to economize to keep up with repayments. With recession, many are unable to cope, and huge numbers of homes are repossessed by the lenders.

The situation is even more precarious in developing countries. Here, millions of families live in unsafe and unsanitary homes, with no latrines, electricity, or clean water. Millions more live in homes built of sacking or cardboard, and in areas prone to flooding, cyclones, or earthquakes. Most people in poor countries have to build their own homes. In this task, extended families may exchange labour, building each other's dwellings in turn. Few poor families have housing rights or legal title to property. In cities especially, eviction is common; sometimes with violence and without warning. For example, in preparation for the 1992 anniversary of Columbus's landing in the Dominican Republic, the major urban centres of Santo Domingo and Santiago were transformed – and "beautified" – by the forced evictions of more than 15,000 families.

"Food not only keeps the family alive, it also underpins its faith"

Countless poor families are simply homeless. They sleep on the streets, under bridges, and on building sites. Wrapped in blankets or newspapers, they huddle together for warmth. They prepare and eat their food out in the open. The luckier ones have a room in a hostel for the homeless or "squat" in an empty building. The spectre of homelessness stalks even the wealthy cities of the industrialized nations. With no home, the physical deprivations are obvious: lack of privacy and exposure to extreme weather, theft, and violence. Less obvious are the social consequences. Homeless people are often disqualified from state benefits and employment. Homeless parents feel deeply anxious about being unable to provide for their children. Being homeless attacks the very fabric of family life.

Of the activities that centre on the home, the preparation and eating of food is crucial. It not only keeps the family alive, but also underpins its faith. It is sustenance in a material and a spiritual sense. For example, North American Indians would

• 10% of the population of the EC countries are homeless or are not secure in their homes (European Parliament committee).

• Canada, with 1.7, has the lowest number of persons per household (Euromonitor).

• North Yemen, with 8.7, has the highest number of people per dwelling.

All over the world, families can be found labouring together, especially in agricultural economies. The Peruvian market (above) sells the produce of family enterprise.

 The most efficient US farms, an Iowa study found, were family-owned and no more than 200 hectares in size (Food First).

burn food to send to a spirit to persuade him to spare the life of a dying child. We share food, and demonstrate intimacy, friendship, and hospitality. We hold elaborate feasts, and thereby display our social status. We devise rituals of eating and fasting, such as Christmas lunch, Thanksgiving dinner, or fasting in daylight hours during Ramadan, that celebrate our faith and our sense of unity.

Families not only raise children, live together, eat together, and share sadness and joy; they also work together. The family has always been the main unit of production in agricultural economies. Among hunter-gatherers and peasant farmers, in craft workshops, and in businesses such as retailing and cater-ing, the family is often a work and income-generating group. This role can be crucial to a family's survival, particularly for the very poor and female-headed households.

There are advantages in using family labour. Children who work alongside their relatives learn important life skills, and working together reinforces family unity. In Europe, for example, the divorce rate is lower in farming and in trades where the family works together. Possibly this is because partners own assets jointly and share the workload, making divorce econom-ically painful. Also, in communities using family labour, out-ward mobility is low and traditional values strong, making it harder for couples to divorce.

In the Peruvian Andes family labour is a vital part of the agricultural economy. Here, farming techniques are primitive and labour-intensive. Brothers and sisters from one family marry siblings from another, forging multiple marriage bonds between two sets of relatives. These ties bolster the labour of individual households. For example, while one of the women pastures ani-mals belonging to herself and others in her family, her mother, or mother-in-law, will look after her children while her sister collects firewood. Most of the year the men work in their own fields, sometimes helped by an older son.

During busy periods, such as harvest time, the various households work together, tending each other's fields in turn. The family forms a tightly knit team and work is allocated by age and gender. All able-bodied members must work, whether they are paid or not, in the home, fields, or the family business. Elderly members cook, tend animals, or care for infants.

The burden of family labour can fall heavily on some members. In Africa, for example, more than 90 per cent of all food is grown by women and children. Individual welfare is sometimes sacrificed to the welfare of the group as a whole. Children may be "bonded", working in slavery to repay family debts to employers. Others work as prostitutes so that earnings can be remitted to their parents.

In industrial economies the family no longer plays a direct role in economic production. Extended families are dispersed and the smaller nuclear family is independent. The knowledge and work skills contained in the family are inadequate in the face of advanced technologies and specialized occupations. Mechanization has replaced much of the work done by unskilled family members and the mass market has taken over a large

The Gimi at work
The Gimi people of Papua New Guinea divide their domestic and work arrangements according to gender. The men and initiated boys live together in men's houses. Women live with their mothers-in-law or co-wives. Within fenced gardens, women care for infants, raise livestock, and grow food, while men work in teams to clear forest and construct the boundaries within which women are confined. Men's work is seasonal and sporadic, while women's is steady and repetitive throughout the year.

number of the productive tasks once provided within the household, which has reduced people's reliance on one another. In the industrialized world, the family is now more important as a key unit of consumption, rather than production.

The family protects and transmits human values and cultural identity, passing on religious convictions and historical traditions from generation to generation. But in preserving the past, it can also help perpetuate attitudes which harm some family members, such as the denial of equal rights for women.

The family is also a major conveyor of wealth from generation to generation. Ties of marriage and descent are vested with more than a common interest in offspring; there is also the desire to reinforce family status by accumulating material goods. The right to property and its transfer either within or between families is the subject of ancient and often strict custom, usually regulated by law. Not surprisingly, much conflict within families focuses on the control of wealth. Property interests can expose the darker side of family life, such as the rivalry between siblings contesting a will.

Most property transfer within the family occurs at a marriage or a death; sometimes smaller gifts mark a child reaching adulthood. Women may receive their share at marriage – the dowry payment – enabling them to bring assets such as cash or jewellery to the new household. Men, though, are more likely to receive their share of family wealth at the death of their parents. Where fragmentation of the family's fund could be economically disastrous, there may be only one heir – usually either the eldest or youngest son.

In most cultures men control the property. Men are also the more powerful, even where funds are ostensibly allocated to women. The property a woman receives from her father, for example, is often passed on to her husband. Frequently, though, men and women inherit different kinds of property. From their mothers, women receive personal items and goods useful in the home, such as kitchenware, subsistence animals, and even houses and subsistence plots. Men are more likely to inherit goods from which an income may be earned, such as fields suitable for cash crops, trees, family businesses, vehicles, and working animals.

Because property transfers are a major part of marriage, divorce too tends to feature complex negotiations over valued

Families and farmland
Between 1976 and 1979 the University in Krakow, Poland, carried out research on traditional inheritance systems. The survey covered 6 villages, comprising 1800 farms with an average size of 5 hectares. All children have a legal entitlement to the family farm, although farms below 8 hectares cannot be legally divided. However, the custom of "paying off" non-inheriting siblings remains a major form of regulating intra-familial obligations – half of non-inheriting urban children received financial aid and 63% received occasional food supplies .

the inheritor

The flow of wealth from one generation to the next is often subject to ancient custom. At a Sikh wedding in the US (above), guests give presents of money to the bride and groom. Couples are sometimes betrothed at a very young age.

Guests at a betrothal ceremony in Myanmar (right) affix money to a fruit plant. This symbolizes the families' and community's investment in the new union – the hope that it will grow and bear fruit.

goods. In the West, specialized divorce lawyers fight long, hard battles in and out of court to obtain divorce settlements of sometimes truly staggering proportions.

Property transfer has a significant impact on the preferences parents have for the gender of their children. In the European and Asian dowry systems, daughters take a substantial portion of family property with them at marriage, and must shift their allegiance to their in-laws. Daughters are, therefore, very costly and the preference is for sons. The inflation of dowry payments in some societies has reached such a pitch that female fetuses, identified by amniocentesis, are aborted. To many parents the costs of these medical procedures are insignificant when compared with the daunting prospect of saving for years to pay for the dowry. Property relations, it would seem, can crucially affect human reproductive behaviour and the prospects of individual members.

Safeguarding the individual

Some family members can never leave home or establish an independent life. This may be due to illness or disability; it may be due to infirmity in old age. In the absence of wider support, the family provides a safety net for those unable to care for themselves. Indeed, the family is the most important welfare institution in the world.

Care-giving takes patience, courage, and energy. Mothers usually take principal responsibility for caring for a disabled child, and daughters, more often than sons, look after an aged parent. Few family carers have any respite from their responsibilities. In many cases their greatest problem is economic. Families often take on financial hardship in providing for a member who will never contribute to domestic income.

It is AIDS, however, that threatens all the usual welfare roles of the family. Projections for Central and East African countries suggest that in the 1990s more than 5 million children will be orphaned by AIDS. Many children are having to care for sick or dying parents. Elderly people become parents again as they care for orphaned grandchildren. In these regions the extended family has traditionally cared for orphans, but their numbers have become too vast. Countless children have been left in hospitals and orphanages, or have drifted onto city streets.

In industrialized countries, the family's first-aid role has changed with the decline of the extended family and the increase in the workforce's mobility. Families are dispersed, often leaving the elderly isolated from their adult children in times of need, and also unable to provide support when, for example, a grandchild is ill. An array of specialist services provide for individual welfare, including hospices for the terminally ill, homes for the elderly, and special schools for handicapped children.

In some countries, policy changes and cuts in public spending have caused a serious welfare crisis. For example, programmes to empty institutions have thrown vulnerable, dependent people suffering from mental disorders onto the streets of major cities such as New York and London. This welfare crisis shows the danger of relying too heavily on the state. The family

Child poverty in Italy

A 1990 study by the Innocenti centre on "Child poverty and deprivation in Italy" found that the number of children in institutions fell by half between 1975 and 1983 to 56,099. The decrease was due in part to Italy's declining fertility rate, but also to the growth of support services for the family, and the increase in foster care. The proportion of children in care from the South and the islands, however, rose due to the greater poverty and lack of foster homes.

● 5 million UK adults care for an elderly or infirm relative (UK government).

● Half of all UK carers have dependants aged 75 or over.

● 53% of UK carers look after parents or parents-in-law.

the safety net

Yamunavathi, a pupil at a school for the physically handicapped in Bangalore, India, gets a lift to the school bus from her brother (left).

can provide a more effective and less expensive safety net than government. Formal institutions rarely offer the warmth and love of a family. Yet the demands on family are many. Without some assistance from the state, families are unable to fulfil their many roles effectively.

When the world outside is full of pressures, when it is threatening and uncertain, people have an instinctive urge to retreat. They need to withdraw to where life is stable and predictable, where somebody loves them, and where there is emotional support. As the mother's body provides the first protection to the developing child, so the family provides a supportive boundary around its members – a "haven in a heartless world".

In the informal and intimate setting of the family, a sense of solidarity, warmth, and trust develops. We express these intimacies verbally and non-verbally, through gestures, expressions, and songs. Much communication within the family is casual, and often it seems incidental. The simple moments of family life, as when the family is relaxing at the end of the day, are profoundly comforting and reassuring to its members.

In most societies it is mothers who provide the caring for infants. Because they spend a considerable amount of time together, mothers and children get to know each other well and develop close emotional ties. These ties are a powerful source of happiness and identity for all. Family relations are emotionally charged. Love and affection, anger and aggression, all find expression. Emotional expression is a deeply important part of children's development, and it is encouraged through play.

Often it is during their leisure time that family members are most intimate with each other. Indeed, providing recreation is a key role of the family. Traditionally, play is relaxed, informal, and spontaneous, contrasting strongly with work or school. Television has become the main recreational tool in most homes in the West where children spend as many hours watching television as they do at school. Many people are concerned that television is harmful to family life; family members spend more time watching television and less time in other activities or conversation. The television is perhaps the modern day replacement for the hearth, where the family would gather, talk, and entertain each other. A nostalgia for this age persists, illustrating the family's focus as a place to belong, to be supported, to find affection.

In the Amazon rainforest a Yanomami elder relaxes, enjoying a quiet moment with his children and grandchildren (above).

the great supporter

*"Much communication within the family is casual,
and often it seems incidental"*

a world of families

The family lives. The family evolves. For thousands of years it has adapted to a constantly changing world. Instead of "the family", perhaps we should speak of "families", since the forms vary so much within regions and between cultures. The following pages explore how these diverse forms are as different as they are alike.

There is no simple view of the family; no universal definition. Most of us assume we know exactly what one is. We might say that it is a household, a group of people who live together under the same roof – and who are related. But this section shows that a family is more than this; it is not always tied to one place and to one time. A family may be split between households. Its members may have no biological link between them.

Economic, technological, and social developments are having a powerful impact on families. A growing number of couples do not have children; perhaps as many as a third of families have only one parent; and some centre on the partnership of two adults of the same sex. Do these new families indicate a decline in the worth of the family? Or do they show how families are developing to meet the challenges of the modern world?

Rite of passage: almost every culture marks the transition from childhood to adulthood with a special ritual or religious ceremony. The bar mitzvah of Jewish culture (left) is deeply important for this boy and his family.

Nuclear and extended families

The image of "the family" conjured up by the media is a household of husband and wife, with their dependent children. This nuclear group is found worldwide, but it is most prevalent in the West where it seems to epitomize the "modern" family. With its cycle of children growing up, leaving their parents, and starting their own nuclear group, it has become the image of "the family" in the popular imagination and in government policymaking. It is a powerful model to which people aspire, and a standard by which they judge themselves and others. Yet even in a Western country such as the UK, little more than a quarter of all households take this form.

Nuclear families are commonest in industrialized cities, from Tokyo to Brasilia, Cape Town to Stockholm. We assume that industrialization created them, yet small nuclear families lived in European towns for centuries before the industrial revolution. In urban England before the nineteenth century, it is believed that nine out of every ten homes contained a nuclear family. People did not marry until their late twenties, and their own parents might have died in their early forties. There was little chance for the three generation, extended family to emerge. With the advent of industrialization, adult life expectancy increased, so three generation families became common in towns and cities.

In more recent years, increased modernization and industrialization has generally led to families becoming more geographically and socially mobile, with the result that extended family ties are shed. Modern industrial and urban living is tending to erode family structures back into the more isolated nuclear form. The more that families become isolated from their

nuclear families

The small, nuclear family from Nicaragua (above) must survive without the extra labour normally provided in rural areas by an extended family. The family from Sudan (left) is more typical of Africa where extended families predominate.

Family break-up in India

Quarrels within a rural Indian extended family can result in its gradual break-up, and the creation of nuclear families. A couple and their children may set up individual hearths and build walls to divide a courtyard. A rebellious nuclear group might even move house taking furniture and cattle, but will still farm with the extended family.

In Japan, the family has undergone many changes since the end of the Second World War and the country's rise to economic supremacy.

The traditional pattern of household formation was the "stem" family system, founded on a belief in lineal continuity from one generation to the next. One son was the successor to family headship and heir to family property. He lived in his parent's home, which subsequently became the home of his wife and children.

During the past 50 years a new "conjugal family" system has grown. This focuses on the marital bond; each couple lives in an independent household, separate from parents and married children.

Under the stem family system, nuclear households were not uncommon. The rise of the conjugal family system, however, has meant a corresponding rise in nuclear households. The rapid growth of the Japanese economy between 1960 and 1975 gave further impetus to nuclearization, as young people had greater opportunities for employment and supporting their own households.

The stem family system has not disappeared – but it is less common today. Most elderly people still live in kin households. The proportion of the old living with their family fell from 87% in 1960 to 66% in 1980. In parallel, the percentage living in married-couple, single-person, and institutional households has risen.

grandparents and other relatives, the more they become reliant on state and private support. This vulnerability of the nuclear family means that when it is under stress, it cannot guarantee quality of life for its individual members.

When people speak of "the family" in the West, they tend to refer to children being reared by parents until they leave home to start their own family. To most of the rest of the world, though, individuals do not begin families; they are born into them, and stay in them until old age and death – or even beyond.

An "extended family" generally contains more than two generations; parents, grandparents, and children. It might also contain aunts, uncles, and other more distant relatives. These families are vital in rural areas where they are often the backbone of agricultural production. They are a useful means of pooling labour when it is needed – and when there is no money to pay for it. Frequently, this family form is linked to the availability of food. For example, in lowland regions of the Amazon, indigenous families congregate in villages at the river's edge during the wet season, when there are fish in the water and fruits in the forest. During the dry season they disperse in search of retreating food supplies.

The joint family

Typical of rural families in India and until recently in Russia and the Balkans, the joint family contains two or more married couples, and their children, living under the same roof. This form of extended family maximizes the labour available in regions where land is not yet scarce or a marketable commodity. Its largest expression was the Zadruga group, common in the Baltic in the nineteenth century. Up to 80 people lived together, usually married brothers and their families.

extended families

In Africa, nuclear families are in the minority. Indeed, in North Africa, the average size of households in cities appears to be increasing, probably because of housing shortages. Elsewhere in Africa, living arrangements comprise of more than the biological family nucleus, for reasons that include kinship networks, polygamy, and the taking in of divorced women and widows. Migrants to towns add to these enlarged families as they often stay for long periods of time with urban relatives.

The need of the extended family to protect the entire kin group takes priority over the individual's concerns. This can make life hard for the powerless and weak. Yet extended families have many strengths: they provide succour for their abandoned and orphaned, they collaborate, and they share.

Embedded in Western marriage is the notion that at any one time a person can have only one spouse. In some traditional societies, however, polygamy is an option that can influence relations between spouses.

"Polygyny" – marriage between one man and two or more women – often flourishes where land is plentiful, infant mortality is high, and women produce much of the food – as in sub-Saharan Africa. Indeed, the more that women participate

"Individuals are born into families, and stay in them until old age and death – or even beyond"

The family is central to African society. It varies greatly in form and size; nuclear families exist, but extended families predominate.

In traditional African society, a woman usually lives with her husband's family after marriage. Their children become the responsibility of the entire family group. The extended family in which sons live together with their wives and children in one compound is less common today. However, solidarity with kin continues, in forms adapted to new economic circumstances.

Statistics suggest an increasing incidence of the so-called "enlarged nuclear household"; a central family unit whose numbers are swelled by distant family members. Migrants may spend long periods with relatives, and small-scale enterprises often depend on the labour provided by the extended family.

A phenomenon in sub-Saharan Africa is the stability of polygamy, particularly in rural areas where women are central to production. Notable, too, is the high incidence of women moving in and out of marriages. By the age of 50, about half of all women have seen an end

to their first union, as a result of separation or widowhood. Remarriages are more common in sub-Saharan Africa than in North America.

The continent has suffered enormous economic pressures in recent decades, which could have destroyed the traditional concepts of the family. Yet the idea of a family as more than just parents and their children has shown remarkable resilience.

Polyandry – where a woman has more
than one husband – is a relatively rare
phenomenon. It may be found in
several regions, including the
Himalayas, where this Sherpa woman
and her two husbands live (above).

in production, the greater the number of polygynous men. By bringing more than one wife into the family, a man gains an abundance of female labour, and in the longer term benefits from the labour of many children. Land in Africa is worth little and so men do not try to accumulate large properties by limiting the number of heirs. Paternity suits are likely to involve men claiming heirs, whereas disowning heirs is the common practice in many other parts of the world.

Women marry early and men late, ensuring that there are more women than men available for marriage, and that men are likely to have greater social and economic status to support many wives. The age difference also ensures that women are widowed relatively frequently, increasing the total number available for remarriage. Indeed, polygyny facilitates remarriage. Sometimes it is customary for a widow to marry another member of her husband's kin.

Traditionally, the co-wives work interdependently as this favours their agricultural and domestic work. Some cultures relieve any tension between wives by establishing separate households for each, arranged around a clearing or courtyard. Often however, the husband is not wealthy enough to maintain such an arrangement, and wives share the same house, and even the same bedroom. Among most polygynous peoples the majority of men can afford no more than one wife; the poorest can afford none.

"Polyandry" – where a woman has more than one husband – is far rarer than polygyny. Yet polyandrous peoples are found as far apart as the Marquesas Islands in the Pacific Ocean and the foothills of the Himalayas. The Nyinba people of Nepal and the Todas of southern India practise fraternal polyandry, where the husbands are brothers. Polyandry makes it hard to detect biological fathers, but the social bond of paternity is always acknowledged. Today men assert fatherhood in a ceremony in which one of the husbands gives a miniature bow and arrow to the wife during her pregnancy. The advantage of brothers marrying the same woman is that it keeps them together so the land handed down to them by their father is not divided, and may be passed on to the next generation. Occasionally, a group of sisters will marry a group of brothers.

Although unfamiliar to people who practise monogamous marriage, multiple unions often make economic sense. Polyandry is an ingenious strategy for societies to adapt to the scarcity of good land and resources. It harnesses the work of a

polygamous families

Polygamy USA
Polygamy in the USA is illegal. However, in certain Mormon communities polygyny is practised. The founder of the Mormon church, Joseph Smith, was persecuted for advocating polygyny, which was common among Mormons in the nineteenth century. Today, polygyny is less widespread, but in the spiritual home of the Mormons, Salt Lake City, many men still defy the law and are married to more than one woman. Elsewhere, in isolated areas of Montana and Arizona, closed Mormon communities flourish with polygynous marriages commonplace.

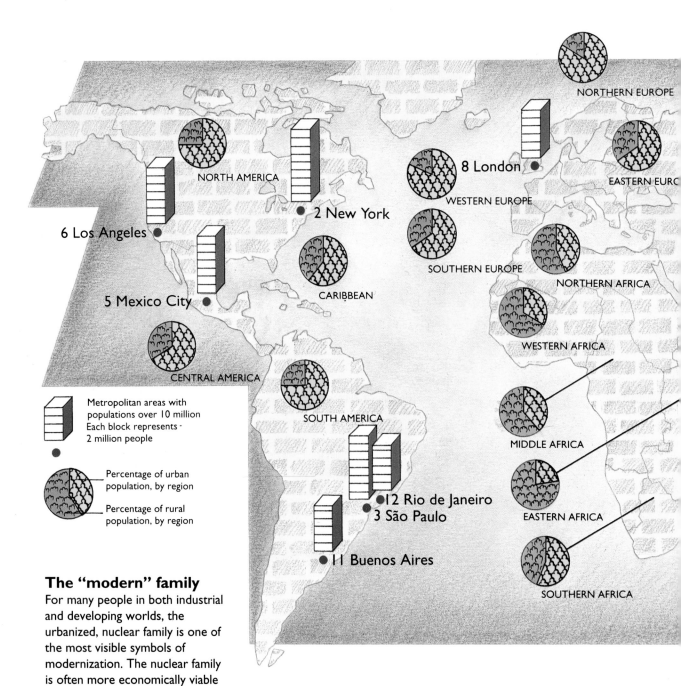

NORTHERN EUROPE

NORTH AMERICA

WESTERN EUROPE

8 London

EASTERN EURC

6 Los Angeles

2 New York

SOUTHERN EUROPE

NORTHERN AFRICA

5 Mexico City

CARIBBEAN

WESTERN AFRICA

CENTRAL AMERICA

SOUTH AMERICA

MIDDLE AFRICA

12 Rio de Janeiro
3 São Paulo

EASTERN AFRICA

11 Buenos Aires

SOUTHERN AFRICA

Metropolitan areas with
populations over 10 million
Each block represents ·
2 million people

Percentage of urban
population, by region

Percentage of rural
population, by region

The "modern" family

For many people in both industrial and developing worlds, the urbanized, nuclear family is one of the most visible symbols of modernization. The nuclear family is often more economically viable than the extended group, which has become less frequent in the majority of cities. Rural-to-urban migration frequently reinforces this pattern. Census data, for example, shows that 80% of migrants to Indian cities settle in nuclear families rather than the traditional joint family system.

number of men to support a family. It also limits family size by having one wife to bear children. Nyinba women frequently say that they prefer to have more than one husband since it gives them greater economic security.

During the 1990s, more than 80 per cent of global population growth will take place in cities. Already, half of humanity is urbanized and even where relatively few live in cities – as in much of Africa – migration from rural areas is changing the shape and behaviour of families.

urbanizing families

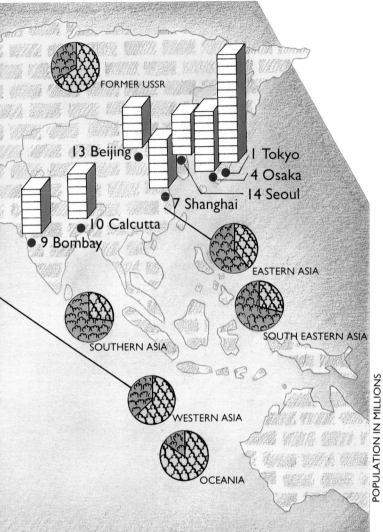

13 Beijing

1 Tokyo

4 Osaka

14 Seoul

7 Shanghai

10 Calcutta

9 Bombay

FORMER USSR

EASTERN ASIA

SOUTH EASTERN ASIA

SOUTHERN ASIA

WESTERN ASIA

OCEANIA

About half the world's people live in towns and cities. There are now 14 hyper-cities with more than 10 million people each (left). Ten of these are in the developing world, where in 1950 there were none. Urban areas swell not only with their own population increase, but with the migration from rural regions. The future looks even more urban. During the 1990s, more than 80 million people a year will be added to the world's cities. The graph (below) shows the UN projection for rural and urban global populations – by 2025, about two-thirds of all people will be urbanized.

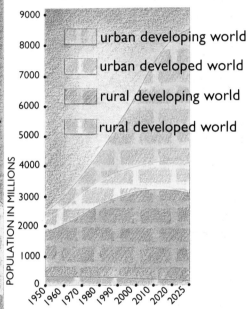

POPULATION IN MILLIONS

9000
8000
7000
6000
5000
4000
3000
2000
1000
0

urban developing world

urban developed world

rural developing world

rural developed world

1950 1960 1970 1980 1990 2000 2010 2020 2025

"More than 80 per cent of global population growth will take place in cities"

Family life in cities often requires a mobile and flexible workforce, not one tied down by an extended family. The cost of living is high, and it is expensive to educate children. It is hard to sustain large families, and nuclear groups are beginning to prevail. Rural-to-urban migration often reinforces this pattern.

Everyday throughout the world, thousands of people migrate to urban areas in search of a job, education for their children, or the bright lights and excitement. Migrant families from the country frequently settle in the nuclear rather than the traditional form and others travel alone. Families are then split over great distances – lone parent families are sometimes created.

● Between 1950 and 1990 the world's urban population more than trebled (UN).

● Africa has the highest annual rate of urban growth - it has remained above 4.5% since 1950 (UN).

● 40% of urban Indians live 5 to a room (UN).

In a recent US census, 27% of all families with children are headed by a single-parent. The census confirms that "the family" is no longer easy to define. Among "family-based households", once-conventional nuclear families of married couples with children are now slightly less common than childless couples.

Two main trends account for the high incidence of lone parenthood. About half of all marriages end in divorce; and the number of never-married women having children is steadily rising.

Whatever their nationality single-parent families are most vulnerable to economic hardship. Each has to survive on the income of one adult, who may experience difficulties in single-handedly combining the roles of caretaker and breadwinner. More than half of the families living below the poverty line in the US are female-headed. Women's average incomes fall substantially after divorce, while men's rise by up to 73%. Although men are required to pay maintenance, many fail to do so. Single, teenage mothers are often in the worst plight; almost 90% are living below the poverty line.

Lone carers

Today, between one-quarter and one-third of all households are headed by a single parent. Lone parenthood has always been a major part of family life. In the past, early death in adulthood was one of its main causes. In pre-industrial Europe, for example, widowhood was a common experience, due to frequent wars or epidemics; many were widowed three or four times. Nowadays, adult mortality is still a serious problem in poor countries in crisis, but in general, improved living standards and health care ensure adults live longer than in the past. Today, high rates of separation and divorce, migration, and births to women without partners are the major causes of single-parent families. Most people are driven into single parenthood, but for many it is only a temporary arrangement until they remarry.

Life is difficult for the single parent, especially the single mother, not least because of prejudice and social stigma. The sheer physical and emotional fatigue of raising children alone, and trying to be the main source of both affection and authority at the same time, drains morale. Lone teenage mothers are more vulnerable than most because early child-bearing can cause health complications, poverty, and social rejection. Their children are likely to be underweight for their age, and malnourished. Lone fathers fare better than lone mothers. Friends, relatives, and neighbours are more likely to rally around, and their living standards are usually higher.

Nine out of every ten lone parents are women. Men can move more freely in and out of parenting relationships than women; they can decline involvement in the maintenance, nurture, and upbringing of their children. In many cultures, male partners are often transient members of the household

In wealthier parts of the world, some economically-independent women are now choosing parenthood without a partner. To these women single parenthood presents new challenges and new opportunities.

Between 20 and 30 per cent of households in the industrialized world, Africa, Latin America, and the Caribbean are headed by women. Most are either lone parents, heads of extended families, or elderly women living alone. In contrast, women in Asia and the Pacific are unlikely to head families. Here, widows, divorcees, and lone women are often absorbed into extended family households.

single parents

In rural Lesotho, 70% of households are headed by women, who manage children, homes, and agriculture on their own (above).

 In Lesotho survival is in the hands of women – the widows of gold. Most men have been lured to the gold mines of "the Neighbour" – South Africa – where average monthly wages are around $280, compared with $16 in Lesotho. Few manage to come home more than once or twice a year or send their wives money.

Widows in all but name, 70% of rural women are left behind to manage homes, look after children, cultivate land, trade produce, and cope with crises.

Development agencies now realize that women farmers are good at managing business and repaying credit, but they need their husbands' permission to obtain the credit. Women remain lifelong minors in a society where their legal status lags far behind their practical responsibilities.

Pragmatic and resourceful, the women are striving to improve their lot. In the village of Hasitoke, 12 women run a poultry-raising and handicrafts co-operative, with initial funds for training and equipment provided by UNICEF. For Matummisang Moteboka, with seven children and no land of her own, the co-op is a lifeline. "My husband works for the Neighbour. I am quite lucky because he comes home once a month. But things can still be very hard for me. I don't make much money from the chickens...but it helps."

"The Neighbour" has imposed sexual apartheid on Lesotho. With few work prospects other than the mines, boys rarely progress beyond the most basic education. Lesotho is one of the few countries where more women than men are literate. From the age of eight, boys spend ever-

increasing periods in the mountains herding cattle, separated from families and an education, before they head for the mines.

Women such as Matummisang are anxious about their children's future. Lesotho is dependent on "the Neighbour", which is beginning to limit migrant labour. They know, too, that their own fragile land is suffering from serious soil erosion. UNICEF is backing the "each one, teach one" scheme – encouraging literate children to teach their friends. However, Lesotho's beleaguered families also need long-term strategies, national and international, to aid their survival.

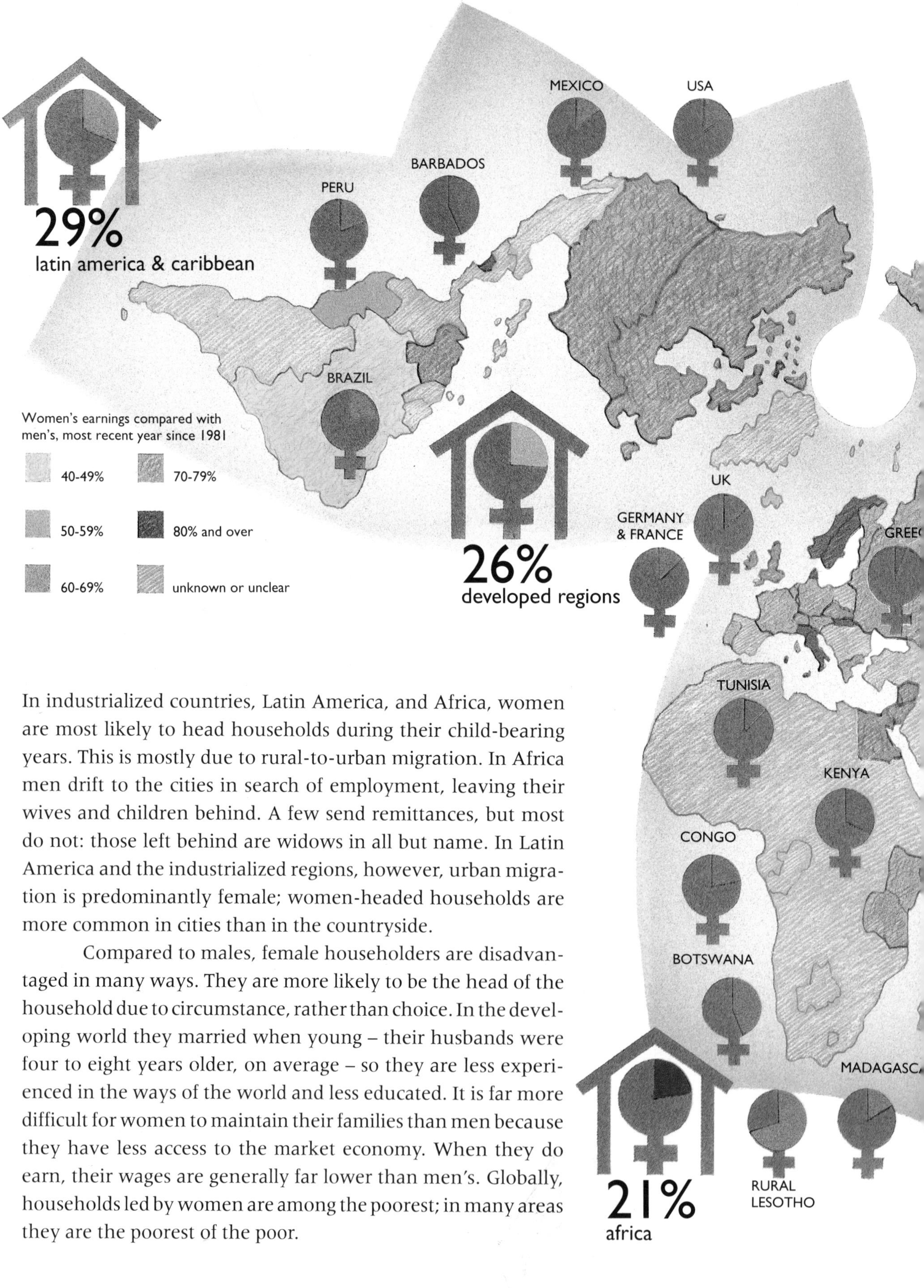

29%
latin america & caribbean

MEXICO

USA

BARBADOS

PERU

BRAZIL

Women's earnings compared with
men's, most recent year since 1981

	40-49%		70-79%
	50-59%		80% and over
	60-69%		unknown or unclear

26%
developed regions

UK

GERMANY
& FRANCE

GREECE

TUNISIA

KENYA

CONGO

BOTSWANA

MADAGASCA

RURAL
LESOTHO

21%
africa

In industrialized countries, Latin America, and Africa, women are most likely to head households during their child-bearing years. This is mostly due to rural-to-urban migration. In Africa men drift to the cities in search of employment, leaving their wives and children behind. A few send remittances, but most do not: those left behind are widows in all but name. In Latin America and the industrialized regions, however, urban migration is predominantly female; women-headed households are more common in cities than in the countryside.

Compared to males, female householders are disadvantaged in many ways. They are more likely to be the head of the household due to circumstance, rather than choice. In the developing world they married when young – their husbands were four to eight years older, on average – so they are less experienced in the ways of the world and less educated. It is far more difficult for women to maintain their families than men because they have less access to the market economy. When they do earn, their wages are generally far lower than men's. Globally, households led by women are among the poorest; in many areas they are the poorest of the poor.

"Households led by women
are among the
poorest of the poor"

14%
asia & pacific

women-headed households

INDONESIA

PAKISTAN

SRI LANKA   THAILAND

IRAN

Women-headed households are a growing phenomenon. They make up between a quarter and a third of all households (left). In the industrialized regions, a majority of women-headed households consist of women living alone – half of these are elderly. In the developing world the majority include children or other dependants. In all regions, since there is only one provider and women's earnings are less than men's, a disproportionate number of these households live in poverty.

Average percentages of women-headed households in selected countries (left) and per region (right) Percentages for individual developed countries refer only to households containing children

Why so many women-headed households?
● About half the women householders in Africa, Asia, the Pacific, and the industrialized regions are widowed. This is generally due to the trend for women to marry older men in most developing regions, and to greater female longevity.
● In the industrialized countries, the increase in separation and divorce is largely behind the growth in female-headed families.

● Many developing world husbands migrate to the towns or other countries in search of greater earnings. Wives are left with even more family and economic responsibilities.
● Temporary, or "visiting", relationships are common in many regions. In South Africa, for example, male migrants working in towns tend to form temporary relationships with women.

❝I go home at night, but I work here every day so that I can earn enough to pay my mother for food and clothes. I have two sisters, both younger, and I am in charge of them while we are begging on the street."

Now aged 10, Maria has been her family's main breadwinner for three years. Her father is absent and her mother without work. Maria lives in Albania's capital, Tirana, where about 130 children spend their days begging around the city's two hotels.

Albania, the poorest country in Europe, has few street children compared with some parts of the world. But the problem is growing, largely due to economic pressures. Many East European governments have cut services, kept wages down, and removed subsidies on essential items. In Albania, 20% of children are malnourished and infant mortality has doubled since 1989.

"I went to school for three years and would love to go back. I get ill sometimes and then I can't work. I was arrested once and taken to the police station for three hours, but then they let me go. What I need is food and clothes, and someone to take care of me."

Maria is shouldering the responsibility of an adult and missing an education to improve her future. She is living on the margins of society and there is every danger that she will be drawn into the underworld of prostitution and drugs.

Maria told her story to ChildHope, the international charity running health, education, and training projects for street children. Such NGOs are often the only source of help and protection for the vulnerable.

These Chilean girls (above) have been left to fend for themselves following the arrest of their parents.

Murdered street children in Brazil often gain what they were denied in life – a family. Unidentified bodies cannot be given an official burial. So, welfare agencies find families willing to adopt children posthumously, and give them an identity and the right to a decent burial.

Countless children living in war zones or areas of natural disaster, in extreme poverty or where there is social upheaval, do not have the support of families. The plight of Brazil's estimated 7 million street children is better known than most because it has received so much media attention. They survive by their own ingenuity and strength without the help of adults. Often, small groups form a family with its own leader, territory, and even slang. They share food when it is in short supply and take care of each other when sick. For safety and warmth, many sleep nestled together, leaving one person on constant guard against muggers or police raids.

Child-headed families may consist of brothers and sisters who have been orphaned, abandoned, or separated accidentally from their kin. They are the most vulnerable family unit. In Peru, for example, after many years of civil war, the number of child-headed families has increased dramatically. Most are refugees from the fighting in the mountains between Shining Path terrorists and the army. These children now live in the suburban slums of Lima, the capital. Here, they find safety and anonymity, living in small huts on waste land. Many have lost contact with their parents and they eke out a meagre existence by begging, or working as maids and porters. They assume false identities, for fear of allegations that they are Shining Path members. Without proper identification, they cannot attend school or health clinics. Not knowing who to trust, they cannot even turn to neighbours for help.

"Child-headed families are the most vulnerable family unit"

Globally, many children take to living on the streets where they are persecuted and harassed by the police, shopkeepers, and local residents. These hungry and sick children are often drawn into drug and prostitution rings, the latter with the risk of unwanted pregnancies, backstreet abortions, and infection from sexually transmitted diseases. They "belong" to nobody, and children living without adults are easy prey – there is no one to defend them or to mourn their death.

From 1988 to 1992 an extraordinary "family" of 12,500 Sudanese boys wandered the deserts of Sudan, Ethiopia, and Kenya. Some had been orphaned in the civil war in their country. Many, it is thought, had been taken from their families by Sudanese rebel forces, to become soldiers. Accompanied by a few "teachers" - members of the Sudan People's Liberation Army - the boys kept moving; barefoot, they walked 2000 km during their four-year ordeal.

The boys, most of them aged between 10 and 16 years, became adults before their time. They took on the responsibility of caring for each other – for those traumatized by their experiences or suffering from malnutrition-related diseases. They became their own substitute family, providing one another with support and a sense of belonging.

In 1992, the boys finally reached a refugee camp in Kenya, where they have remained. Some boys have been reunited with their families. Others, with help from refugee organizations, are trying to trace their relatives in the hope of rejoining them.

New families

Today's children and young adults are likely to experience different family lives from those of their parents. As average family size decreases, and divorce, lone parenthood, and remarriage increase, an individual can experience several family types during a lifetime.

In the US, for example, divorce rates are among the highest in the world, but remarriage rates are also very high. Anthropologists call this "serial monogamy" – people have multiple spouses, but one at a time. One child in five will experience a parental divorce. Many of these children will temporarily belong to a lone-parent family, but can expect to gain a step-parent, and probably even step-brothers and step-sisters – of a similar age or perhaps of a very large age difference.

Step-families, like foster and adoptive families, have been common throughout history. Despite their many advantages, these "hybrid" family arrangements attract a negative image. They are accused of being less secure, and potentially more damaging to children, than families based on blood ties. Family research in industrialized countries often focuses on such problems as conflict in step-families, or the quest of adoptees to find their biological parents. As might be expected, there are many adjustments to be made in creating step-families. Remarriages, in particular, carry a greater statistical risk of dissolution than first marriages, and some children are abused or neglected by their step-parent. Myth needs to be separated from reality, however; families based on blood ties are not necessarily any healthier or happier. The "reconstituted" family can provide a new kind of extended family with the rich potential for many step- and half-relatives, and the additional support and experience they offer.

Worldwide, children have always experienced a rich diversity of family settings that are not necessarily the result of crises such as orphanhood, divorce, or abandonment. Shared parenting within the extended family or among neighbours is very common. Children who are "exchanged" between households are in effect messengers of family solidarity, helping to maintain the ties of interdependence linking kin. Informal fostering or adopting allows household size and composition to be regulated. Households with too many mouths to feed deliver their children up to childless couples or to families with a shortage of labour. Women beyond child-bearing age may take in foundlings or unacknowledged illegitimate children. Fostering a child also helps a mother with weaning, or frees her to have

• In Lomé, capital of Togo, one in four children aged 10 to 14 lives in a household other than his or her mother's.

• There were 9000 adoptions in the UK in 1989 – less than half the number registered in 1976 (UK Government).

• In 1976, a fifth of all UK adopted children were aged 10 or over; by 1986 the proportion was almost a third.

Family attitudes
In 1992 the Roper Organization polled US citizens on what constitutes a family:
• 75% said that two gay men committed to each other and living together are not a family.
• 37% responded that an unmarried man and woman who cohabit for a long time are not a family.
• 10% said that a married couple with no children is not a family.
• 5% reported that a married couple living with children from a previous marriage is not a family.

"hybrid" families

another child. It can also help to ease some of the problems of polygynous marriages. To avoid the jealousy of a co-wife, the Mende of Sierra Leone may foster a young child with a barren woman or a distant relative.

Half a world away, among Inuit families in the Arctic, adoption is widespread. On the Belcher Islands, Canada, one child in four is adopted. A few families even adopt the children of others at the same time as delivering up their own. The adoptees retain ties with their biological family and often can choose their new "parents".

In industrialized countries, children are fewer and fostering or adoption is only an option in extreme cases. The purpose is not shared parenting, but to provide parents for children in difficulty, and children for the childless. The biological and adoptive parents seldom know each other and contact between them is discouraged. The state now regulates the transfer to a

Adoption provides parents for a child in difficulty – or a child for childless couples – and can bring great happiness to all involved (above).

Family change in the UK
Government statistics indicate family trends in the UK. Between 1979 and 1985 the percentage of children living with both parents fell from 83% to 78%. There has been a corresponding rise in the percentage of children living with their natural mother and a stepfather – from 5% to almost 10% over the same period.

Living in a commune, as an alternative to the family, is not a new phenomenon. Over the centuries members of religious orders, for example, have pooled their worldly goods, and shared aspects of their practical and spiritual lives. This century has seen the growth of a different community, not based on a formal allegiance to a religious faith but on a shared philosophy. Dismissively dubbed "hippy communes" by outsiders, these communities represent a serious attempt to go beyond the limitations of the conventional family unit.

Kim Reefe, a member of the Cennedryss community in South Australia, recalls how it began in 1976. Unusually, the first seeds were sown by a nuclear family – Kim's parents and their four adult offspring – who decided to live together for a year as a "household" rather than a family. They defined a household as "a group of six adults choosing to share a house and all the chores and decisions that go with it". Kim explains, "We did not want to slot back into all the old patterns when we were reunited."

The death of both parents in a family close to them was a sharp reminder of the vulnerability of the nuclear family, and of the absence of the support offered by an extended family. The Reefe household joined with others to form a community, ranging from 8 to 55 in age. According to Kim, there were immediate gains – a sense of purposefulness, sharing, and fun – but many problems, too.

From the outset, Cennedryss has held regular meetings to discuss the challenges of individual and collective responsibility. Decisions are made by consensus. Kim feels that the capacity to work through difficulties derives from a firm commitment to communalism. "From the beginning we have held a 300-year vision. In a world so fragilely poised I hold this vision sacred."

new family. Whereas in the past the family cared for the abandoned or orphaned child, this role has been weakened – one example of where the family and the state can be in conflict.

Many people are attracted to living in a communal settlement. The Findhorn Foundation (above) is the UK's largest "intentional community" with more than 200 permanent members.

Many people choose to live in communal arrangements rather than in homes based around a family. Often, these communities retain nuclear family groups, but cooking, eating, child care, and work are shared. Decisions are made communally and property owned collectively.

utopian alternatives

In the West, communal living has often promised an alternative life style to the perceived greed of capitalism. Hippies in the 1960s "opted out" of the prevalent social order, stressing personal relationships over social obligations. Rejecting material possessions and many of the conventions of family, they entered sexual relationships freely and without commitment. In contrast, many communities are united by moral discipline or abstinence, rather than sexual excess. Such communities include the Shakers and the Amish, puritan groups that settled in America in the nineteenth century.

The kibbutz movement in Israel, which now numbers more than 200 collective settlements, stresses community over family. The early kibbutzim needed as many hands as possible to reclaim land from the malarial swamps in the Jordan valley. Women worked alongside the men, while their children were cared for collectively. On the kibbutz the community, not the family, is the unit of consumption, and the focus of life. In the first kibbutzim shared child-rearing was a key part of creating a collective loyalty. The tendency was to emphasize the community, and so downgrade the importance of the family. In recent

Life in an Israeli kibbutz focuses on the community rather than the family. Shared child-rearing is a key part of the kibbutz life style. While parents work to support the community, their children (above) are cared for collectively

• There are estimated to be more than 350 "intentional communities" in North America.

• There are approximately 50 communes in the UK.

While many childless couples long to have their own children, there are those who see themselves as "childfree". Couples who have decided not to have children stress that life can be perfectly fulfilled and rewarding, and see themselves as complete families. The British Organization of Non-Parents, founded by Root Cartwright (left), supports those who have taken such a decision.

 In vitro fertilization, fertility drugs, and surrogacy all show that society desires the normality of having children. So, too, does the existence of many support groups for the childless.

Yet there are people who see themselves as "childfree" – childless by choice. The existence of a support organization in the UK for such a group proves that opting to be childless in a society brings its own pressures. The British Organization of Non-Parents (BON) promotes non-parenthood as a valid alternative to parenthood. It is not, it insists, anti-children or anti-family. It suggests that the concept of "family" need not imply children. "We are happy with each other. We are a family", BON member Jane Sewel confirms, speaking of her relationship with her husband

.BON argues that childless couples have made a responsible choice in an overpopulated world. By contrast, BON chairman Root Cartwright points out, many people who have children give insufficient thought to the changes involved. They may have children for the wrong reasons – to satisfy the expectations of relatives, or to patch up a failing relationship – or they may simply be doing what everyone else does. "Most people", Root Cartwright says, "put more thought into buying a freezer than having a child".

One of BON's aims is to encourage people to make a conscious, rational decision either for or against parenthood, based on careful thought about the realities of child-rearing. The organization challenges society's romanticization of parenthood and the cultural and media bias against non-parents. Not everyone is suited to parenthood, according to BON.

Many people fear a lonely old age without children. BON points out that a study of old people in homes found that, "the sons and daughters rarely visited, while childless people who had spent their lives pursuing busy careers and cultivating friendships and interests outside the family were visited by a wide range of friends, ex-colleagues, and ex-neighbours."

years there has been a reaction to this as the traditional family group has re-emerged. It used to be customary for parents not to visit their babies in the kindergarten during the day – and for children not to live with their parents. Today, many parents want to play a greater part in child-rearing, and many children now sleep in their parents' quarters.

Many researchers have studied the advantages and drawbacks of being raised in a kibbutz. On the plus side, there are no signs of abuse, bullying, or sex crimes, and little rivalry, jealousy, or possessiveness. On the minus side, kibbutz children often turn out to be relatively unemotional and uncreative, with little sense of individual identity. Some show complete disregard for the idealistic vision that first inspired the movement. Indeed, how to transmit the founding ideals of the group through the generations is a problem for many alternative communities.

In Inuit society children are prized and enjoyed by all; adults are thought to be "lonely" without them. Families everywhere set enormous value on having children, and societies have long been preoccupied with enhancing fertility with charms, potions, prayers, and rites. The world's major religions, such as Islam and Christianity, stress the importance of procreation to marriage, and religious texts often subordinate sexuality to reproduction.

Many couples are unable to have children. The World Health Organization estimates that infertility affects as many as 80 million couples worldwide. Infertility can destroy personal hopes and aspirations. Because of the expectations within the family and society, it can bring great shame. In many countries the stigma of infertility often leads to marital disharmony, divorce, or ostracism by the family and community. In Africa, as in many regions, motherhood represents the main means of improving a woman's social and economic standing.

"Infertility affects as many as 80 million couples worldwide"

Women are often perceived to be fulfilled only when they become mothers; marriages remain "provisional" until a child is born. In the West, childlessness in marriage is becoming a matter of choice. One-third of married couples in the former West Germany are childless – many prefer to be thought of as "childfree". Couples who have taken this decision stress that life without children can be perfectly fulfilled.

childless and "childfree"

Financial concerns can also play an important part in the decision not to have children. In those regions where children begin work when young, they soon start to pay for themselves. In modern Western society children begin to work in their teens – or even later – and rarely do parents benefit from their earnings. Modern child-rearing is extremely expensive. An Australian mother estimated the cost of food, clothes, child care, and other essentials at $80,000 to rear a child until age twelve. She reckoned to have spent $1500 before she even carried her newborn through the door of her home.

Changes in social attitudes and reproductive technologies are resulting in new living arrangements and family forms. Two couples – one lesbian and one gay – living together in the US have begun a loving, if controversial, family after marrying. Gregg and Scott became the sperm donors and co-parents. Baby Connor was born in July 1991 (right).

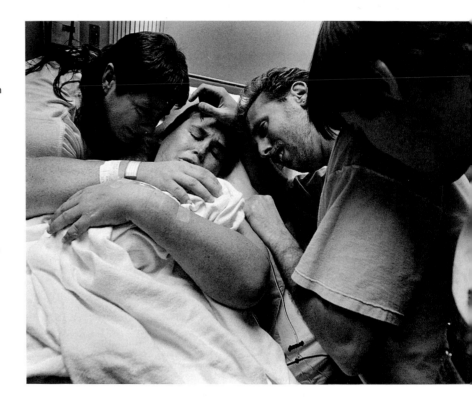

Industrial world families
UNESCO has convened a number of meetings of international experts to reflect on the future of the family. The lack of comprehensive statistical data made it impossible to predict future trends with certainty, but most participants shared the view that the family will remain the basic unit of society. In the industrialized world the following trends were indentified.
● The continued rise of relationships outside marriage, involving various forms of cohabitation.
● The continuing emergence of new family forms, such as single parent and hybrid families:
● A rejection of the concept of communal living.
● As three or more generations are living at the same time, a revival of the "traditional" family is possible.

Domestic organization was once a fairly predictable business; family life was based on biological ties. It was out of these ties that the social bonds of family evolved. However, with modern science this need not apply. Now, more than ever before, family matters are a question of choice rather than kinship loyalties.

Family planning enables couples to choose how many children they want and when to have them. In developing countries the average size of families has reduced from six children in the 1960s to four today. Greater individual freedom makes it possible for single women to raise children alone – with or without the approval of society – and more children look set to live in lone-parent and step-parent families. More people remain single and childless without feeling unfulfilled. More and more people are choosing to "cohabit" and live in relationships that may have great stability but are not marriages, and deliberately lack the commitment and responsibility marriage entails. In Sweden, married couples aged 18 to 24 are outnumbered by those cohabiting.

While cohabitation is an option in heterosexual relationships, many homosexual couples are demanding the social recognition traditionally accorded only to heterosexual marriages. In many countries in the West, it is possible for two men or two women to register as "domestic partners". They are also insisting on the right to raise children – through adoption or the use of reproductive technologies.

"More children look set to live in lone parent and step-parent families"

Remarkable developments in reproductive technologies, such as *in vitro* fertilization (IVF) and embryo and sperm donation and storage, raise a host of new ethical and moral questions concerning the family. Conception can now be an artificial process conducted in a laboratory, without the biological parents being present. Ova or eggs are removed surgically from the woman, mixed with the sperm, and if the eggs develop it is usual for more than one to be placed inside the woman's uterus. A large number of eggs increases the effectiveness of IVF, but it also increases the likelihood of twins and other multiple pregnancies. These are high-risk pregnancies which can place emotional and economic stress on the family. The first such "test-tube baby" was born in 1978. How are the boundaries on experimentation to be set? It is now possible for one woman to donate genetic material, another to bring the fetus to term, and a third to rear the child. What of the legal status of motherhood? Does the frozen embryo have a right to life? If the biological parents divorce who has the right of custody?

No one can predict what effect these reproductive technologies will have on family life. It may be that only a small proportion of people will make use of them. It may be that society will outlaw them. One thing seems guaranteed: the many social and technological forces shaping our lives will create a greater diversity of family forms. Reports of the death of "the family" have been exaggerated.

families of the future

Developing world
Experts on family issues have, at UNESCO's request, identified a number of likely future scenarios for the developing world:
● An increase in the number of Western-style nuclear families in certain social groups, but an end to its adoption as an ideal.
● The maintenance of some forms of the extended family such as the polygamous family in Africa and the joint family in India.
● The family playing a major role in the preservation of cultural identity in the face of Westernization.

family matters

The family is but one of many relationships making up society. But it is unique. This section shows why the family is so different: how it binds its members in a web of social, legal, and economic ties – and also with powerful emotional bonds.

It examines the links in the chain of events that make up family life, the first being the increasingly brittle link of marriage. The family itself changes with the birth and nurture of the young, their growth to adulthood, and the ageing of the founding members. But always it is a living tie between men and women, young and old.

And it explores the ever-increasing concern for the rights and wellbeing of the individual, especially the more vulnerable family members. Each individual in a family affects and influences the other. The wellbeing of one concerns all. And if one member defines his or her role in a new way, the whole family may be transformed.

So will greater equality between men and women alter family life? How will society and families adapt to the call for children's and disabled people's rights? How will we regard the growing numbers of elderly people – as helpless dependants or valuable resources?

Marriage: since time immemorial, individuals and families have been united through matrimony. In India, it is not unusual for girls to be betrothed at an early age; this bride (left) is 4 years old.

Men and women

Worldwide, "living together as man and wife" is still the first choice for the majority of people in search of a supportive relationship, a home, and a family. In many non-Western societies, marriage is virtually a certainty, although it is not always contracted by a public ceremony.

The marital bond is not only expected to fulfil the needs of the individual. Society, too, benefits from it. For thousands of years marriage has provided an ideal opportunity to forge alliances between groups, as well as to secure the future with heirs. It is more than a bond between husband and wife.

There are strong motivations to marry out of the immediate family. Isolated families would have difficulty surviving in the face of competition from groups which create wider networks through the exchange of spouses. Avoiding the biological consequences of incest, too, is an advantage to marrying out. But not too far out. Marriages were – and in many regions still are – prevented if the prospective partner was unknown to the family. One ancient solution is marriage between cousins, which remains popular in Africa and Asia. In some regions of Pakistan and India, up to half of all marriages are between cousins.

Each society arranges and celebrates marriage according to its own customs and traditions. In an Albanian wedding (far right) the bride is required to remain impassive throughout.

In the developing world, women work many more hours than men each day; looking after children, running the home, and tending crops (right).

marriage and partnership

Cousin marriage

Marrying your cousin is banned in 30 states of the US, and is a criminal offence in eight of them. In Asia and much of Africa, however, intermarriage is extremely common. US geneticist James Neel has carried out studies of cousin marriages in Pakistan and India, and suggested that negative Western attitudes to marriage within families are exaggerated. Cousins have an eighth of their genes in common; if they both carry a gene for some genetic disorder, the chance of their child having a pair of such genes – and so having the disease – is high. However, Neel suggests that over many generations, the harmful gene is eliminated. As well as the social and economic advantages of cousin marriage – the girl's parents sometimes do not have to provide a dowry – there may be long-term genetic advantages, too. The practice is likely to become increasingly common. The populations that are growing fastest are also those where cousin marriage is common.

In Japan, married women in full-time employment are rare. A married woman is likely to be a "sengyo-shufu" – full-time housewife – or a "kengyo-shufu" – a housewife who works part-time.

Japan's rise to economic dominance has relied on the male work ethic. It is usual for businessmen to work long hours, six days a week: not a regime conducive to sharing household chores and child-rearing.

The concept of the kengyo-shufu implies some concession to married women's right to work. Typically, the kengyo-shufu looks after her children full-time until they are nearing the end of school. She is then free to seek a job but finds that few are open to her, due to her lack of experience and continuing responsibilities at home. The kengyo-shufu ends up doing manual work that is poorly paid and has little security.

Many Japanese women, equipped with impressive qualifications, are rising to the higher echelons of commerce and industry. However, they are pressurized to work as obsessively as men – or reject the patriarchal work system and become wives and mothers. Until male working hours are reduced and child care services provided, Japanese women will continue having to choose between family and career.

Globally, most societies regard the marital union more as an affair of state than an affair of the heart. Since it performs such a vital function as alliance building, marriages are not arranged by individuals. Neither lust nor love are allowed to interfere, although love is usually expected to follow from the marital union. The classic Asian system is the arranged marriage where matches are determined by the families involved, sometimes as soon as a child is born.

Modern, individualistic values and emphasis on personal choice are gradually eroding the alliance-building role of marriage. In the West, romantic love is seen as the proper foundation for marriage. In celebration of the longevity of marital love the wedding anniversary gift increases in value as the years go by, passing from paper to gold. In China, too, individual choice of a partner, rather than an arranged marriage, has become the general tendency of young people. This was not the case for their parents.

The majority of Western men and women are married by the age of thirty. Half the women in Africa, 40 per cent in Asia, and 30 per cent in Latin America are married by the age of eighteen. In recent years, however, global statistics show that the proportion of married people has fallen, indicating the trend toward later marriage – and an overall decline in marriage in the developed regions.

Even if marriage is less common, this does not mean a movement away from life as a couple. Many people in developed regions, Latin America, and the Caribbean live together – often recognized as "married" in law. The proportion of births to those living outside marriage has increased significantly in countries in all regions. In both Sweden and Belize about half of all births are to unmarried women – although for very different reasons. The proportion of women bearing children without a partner is also growing. Individual choice is creating a huge variety of living and parenting arrangements.

Although different societies have very different views about what qualities are masculine, such qualities are invariably more highly valued than those thought to be feminine. In many societies, men have considerable authority over women. It is the male's family that a bride usually joins. In extreme cases, women lay down their own lives at the death of their husbands. In modern industrial society many old customs have vanished, but signs of them remain: at marriage the father "gives" the bride away; the husband "chooses her hand".

There may not always have been inequality between the sexes. In prehistoric times women were esteemed because of their special relationship with Nature: they created new life; they grew most of the food. Their qualities were the first human ones to be revered in a religious way. Archaeological evidence for fertility and goddess cults suggests that womanhood assumed divine status in the 4000 years between the emergence of the first cultures and the rise of organized religion.

With the replacement of casual cultivation by planned agriculture men gradually took over the tasks that brought in material rewards, while women continued to produce food for the home. Men also discovered their role in reproduction. Fatherhood acquired a political and economic function that developed in parallel with the new beliefs in male gods. Women's work in raising children, producing food, and keeping the home suffered a loss of status.

Today, with men's general monopoly of paid and mechanized labour, official statistics sometimes make it look as if women are not working at all. In reality, women everywhere work more than men – on average, twice as many hours a day in the developing world. The burden of family life falls mostly on women, and their role in producing the goods on which families depend for their survival is often ignored. In many parts of sub-Saharan Africa, for example, women undertake the arduous and heavy agricultural work, in addition to the bearing and caring of children, and running home and family life. Yet it is

women's work, men's work

‘ **Women do not handle the family's income – but they provide labour for most income-generating activities in the home."** So says Elsie Ssekabanja, programme officer at the Mityana women's project in Central Uganda, which helps women work together to improve their income and status.

The women carry an enormous domestic workload; they do all the child-rearing and household tasks; walk three to six kilometres to collect water or firewood; and are also responsible for crops.

"All income is controlled by men", explains Elsie, "so expenditure is determined by husbands. About 80% of rural women are not allowed to run personal activities from which they would earn an income."

Elsie has many stories of men obstructing their wives' initiatives. One woman, whose son had been sent away from school as the fees were behind, decided to earn money by making and selling mats. To pay for the palm leaves and dye, she sold a cockerel – without telling her husband. When he found out, he ordered her to hand over the money or bring the cockerel back.

Another woman planted 50 coffee seedlings in the family plot, traditionally cultivated only with food crops for home consumption. Her husband uprooted the plants and told her she had no right to grow crops for sale.

The Mityana project has found that men can be won over if they see the benefits of women's money-generating activities. Regular visits by community workers can influence men's attitudes. The scheme also seeks to give women more confidence through new skills, and helps them to set up savings and credit groups to run income-generating activities.

men who control the resources of production. Women's access to land is frequently determined by their marital or their inheritance status; in some regions they cannot own property or land, or borrow money.

In industrialized countries, a growing number of women are entering occupations once dominated by men and they are remaining in the workforce following marriage, even with career interruptions for child-bearing. Their working world, however, still differs from men's in type of work, pay, and status.

Women and mothers

Women are more physically resilient than men from birth. Through every decade of life, men are more prone to fatal diseases, and have a lower life expectancy, than women. Despite this, there are fewer women in the world than men, according to UN statistics. In many regions, social and cultural factors deny girls and women the same health care and other essential services, paid employment, and information. This can affect female nutrition, health, income, and mortality. It may keep girls out of school, isolate women from decision-making, and often conditions them to accept their situation.

In the developing world, despite women's longer life expectancy and some significant advances in the past twenty years, their prospects are worse than men's. For every ten boys, there are nine girls enrolled in primary school, but only seven in secondary school. For every ten literate males, there are less than seven females who can read and write. For every ten men in paid employment, there are only five women. In wealthier industrialized countries gaps between men and women have been narrowed in education and health, but they still remain wide in levels of employment and pay. As the UN noted during the Decade for Women (1975-85): "Women comprise about half the world's population, perform about two-thirds of its work, receive only one-tenth of its income, and own less than one-hundredth of world assets."

If women are to realize their full human potential, they will need equality of opportunity with men in health, education, work, resources, and decision-making. To achieve this will clearly require extensive changes in development and government policies, in business, and in the home. It will also require the acceptance that advancing the interests of women benefits everyone. For example, mothers' literacy and infant mortality

Missing women

Although women live longer than men, they make up less than half the world's population. In many countries of Asia and the Pacific there are fewer than 95 women for every 100 men. The reason for this, the UN has shown, is that there are higher death rates for women in poor countries. They generally receive inferior nutrition, health care, and education.

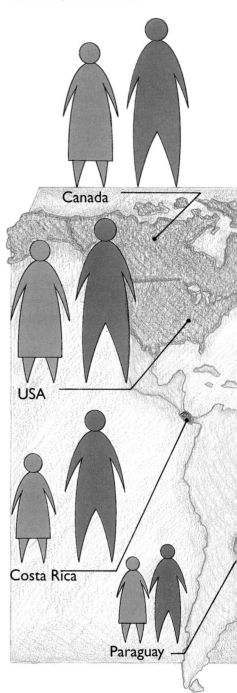

Canada

USA

Costa Rica

Paraguay

"Women comprise about half the world's population, perform about two-thirds of its work, receive only one-tenth of its income, and own less than one-hundredth of world assets"

women in the world

Percentage of women who are literate, for selected countries

- 96-99%
- 90-95%
- 80-89%
- 70-79%
- 60-69%

FEMALE HDI   MALE HDI

Everywhere, there are disparities between men and women. As a relative measure of human progress, the UN has created the Human Development Index (HDI) – a register of social and economic attainment including measures of life expectancy, literacy, and income per citizen for different countries. The height of each figure (below) shows relative HDIs for selected countries – and the disparities between male and female HDIs within countries.

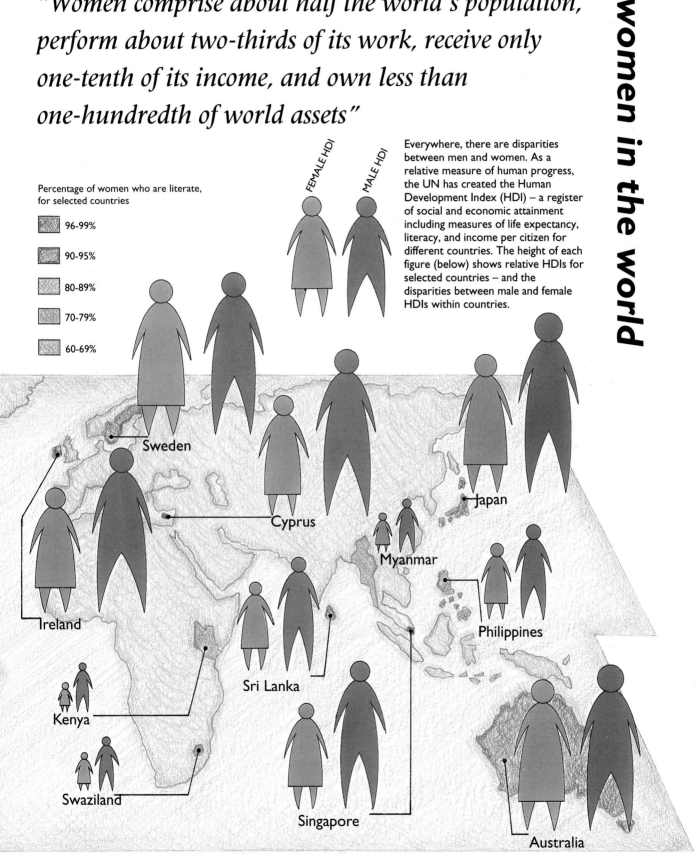

Sweden

Cyprus

Japan

Myanmar

Ireland

Philippines

Sri Lanka

Kenya

Swaziland

Singapore

Australia

are closely related. As the former goes up, the latter comes down. Poor health or low status among mothers also reduces their ability to provide food, fuel, water, and other essentials for the growth and development of their children.

A generation ago the choice for Western parents was often between having three children or four. Today, the choice is more likely to be between having one child or two. In Italy, for example, census data shows that the number of families doubled between 1951 and 1981, but family size dropped by nearly half, to an average of 2.7 people. Nowadays in the West, women have their first child usually in their mid-to-late twenties. Often, the decision to start a family is postponed until the prospective mother is in her thirties.

Two overlapping revolutions have caused this transformation. Modern contraceptive technology is used by an ever increasing number of parents – whatever their religion. Economic prosperity, too, has raised parental expectations, and increased the investment parents feel they must make in each child. Consequently, they have fewer offspring.

In developing countries, however, most parents continue to have many children, and child-bearing starts at an earlier age. Some women are driven to resent the endless succession of pregnancies which affect their health – and they have difficulty in providing for large numbers of children. The World Fertility Survey found that Latin American mothers would prefer to have about three children, not the typical five or six. However, there is poor access to family planning, and many religious and cultural taboos against its use.

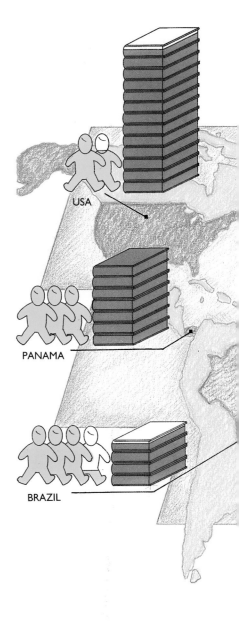

"Latin American mothers would prefer about three children, not the typical five or six"

In the West, women who have children late in life can depend upon modern health care to reduce the risks. Amniocentesis tests, which discover abnormality, are routinely offered to women over 35. The risk of a US woman dying from a pregnancy-related cause is calculated to be as low as 1 in 6400. For an African woman, according to the WHO, the risk is 1 in 21. Complications in pregnancy, childbirth, and unsafe abortions are the leading killers of women of reproductive age in the

Women run the risks
Contraceptive use worldwide is three times greater among women than men, yet female contraceptive methods present higher risks. Most sexually transmitted diseases also have graver medical consequences for women than men (WHO).

reproductive choice

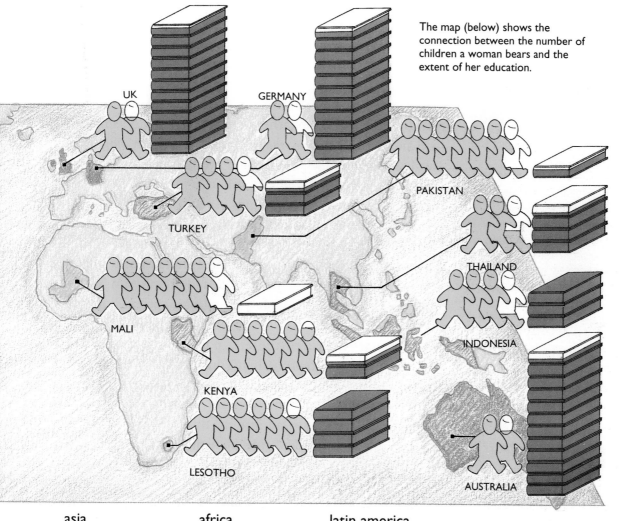

The map (below) shows the connection between the number of children a woman bears and the extent of her education.

UK

GERMANY

TURKEY

PAKISTAN

THAILAND

MALI

INDONESIA

KENYA

LESOTHO

AUSTRALIA

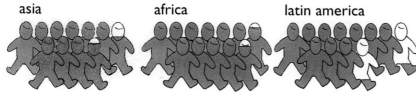

asia

africa

latin america

For the three regions (left), the average number of births to women with no education (top row) is compared to the births to women with 7 or more years of schooling (bottom row).

In the map, the fertility rate per woman is represented by the children (below). The average number of years of schooling for a mother is represented by the height of books. Each book is 1 year.

Maternal mortality per 100,000 live births in selected countries, 1988

0-13		300-400	
50-75		600-850	
180-230			

developing world, causing half a million deaths each year and leaving millions more with ill health or infirmity.

The average age of the first sexual encounter is falling everywhere. In Nigeria, a survey found that 43 per cent of girls aged between 14 and 19 were sexually active. Access to contraception in Nigeria is far less than in a US city such as Baltimore, where three-quarters of high-school students are believed to be sexually active. Pregnancy for those under fifteen years of age is very risky, both for the mother and the baby, with an increased risk of haemorrhaging, anaemia, and permanent reproductive disabilities. Globally, one-quarter of mothers who lose their lives in childbirth are teenagers.

Time with father

A study of four-year-olds in 10 countries discovered that the average daily time spent alone by fathers with their children was less than one hour, ranging from 6 minutes per day in Hong Kong and 12 minutes in Thailand to 54 minutes in China and 48 minutes in Finland. When the average time spent with both parents was added in, the number of hours fathers were present with their children ranged from 1 hour and 36 minutes per day in the US to 3 hours and 42 minutes in Belgium. These findings suggest that even when fathers are present as an active member of a family, their direct involvement in child care can be very limited.

"Fathers should be neither seen nor heard, that is the only proper basis for family life"
Oscar Wilde

Men and fathers

The Mbuti people of north-east Zaire have a beautiful father-hood ceremony. The father has minimal contact with his child until it is two years old. Then the mother carries the child to the father, who holds it to his breast. The baby tries to suck, crying *ema!* (mother!) and the father then gives his child its first solid food and teaches it to say *eba* (father). The anthropologist Colin Turnball suggests that Mbuti men are first perceived by their children as "another kind of mother" – one who cannot give milk but does provide other kinds of food.

Men's own image of themselves as husbands and fathers, and the expectations of them, vary considerably between and within cultures. Generally, many men do not have the opportunity to be loving and caring fathers, and are physically absent from their children for a variety of reasons, such as separation, divorce, or migration to cities or other countries in search of work. Even when living in the same home, many men are absent from the process of rearing their young children. As countries industrialize, the role of fathers in families becomes increasingly tied to work away from home; their role as a socializer of children declines. Studies tend to confirm the male tendency to identify more with the "provider" role than the "nurturer" role, and many feel inadequate in the "woman's domain" of child care and development.

"Studies tend to confirm the male tendency to identify more with the provider role than the nurturer role"

The nineteenth century ideal of the father was a remote but authoritarian figure. Before the industrial revolution much work was done at home, and the family often worked together as an economic unit. The industrial revolution greatly enhanced men's authority in the home. With increased earning power, a man's status was marked by his ability to provide for his wife and children. If his wife was forced to work, he was thought to have failed as a man and as a husband. In most societies today, a man is still expected to "keep" his wife and children: to be the "breadwinner" and the head of the house.

The industrial work ethic is hostile to fatherhood. Men's devotion to work and absence from the home is deemed to be natural. Men are expected to put their work first; the role of the father is seen in relation to the workplace. Few companies plan

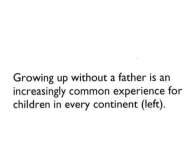

the absent father

Growing up without a father is an increasingly common experience for children in every continent (left).

'Fathers usually provide for the family, and though they buy toys they will rarely play with the children. They have to learn that interaction with their children is important."

Joan Mestres is project director of the Casa de Colors in Barcelona, Spain, where men learn to relate to their children in new ways. Despite Spanish society's image of the father as an authority figure, she believes that some fathers are changing. She cites a recent encounter with a father who attended a story-telling workshop. "The father told me that to him telling stories was like starting a new sport. In the beginning it hurts because you get pain in your muscles; then after some practice, you find you can do it easily. Day after day, as you practise, you enjoy it more."

Enjoyment is also a measure of the success of Father-Child Nights at Escuelita Alegre pre-school in New Mexico, USA. On one night, the men became absorbed in making toys out of scrap wood. The children helped, enjoyed the closeness to their fathers, and showed pleasure at the results. However, as a counsellor gently pointed out, the designs were beyond the developmental stage of the children. The next time, the fathers decided to ask the children how they made toys, to learn how they played, and to let them take the lead.

At the end one boy was heard to say, "Come on Dad, let's go home and play some more". The fathers had been promoted from toy makers to playmates.

for their male employees to become fathers or grant paid paternity leave. Concessions for mothers, such as childcare facilities at work, are denied to fathers.

Some people take father absence as proof that men are not crucial to their children's development. Certainly, vast numbers of well-adjusted and healthy children are raised without fathers – and many are also raised without mothers. Research suggests, however, that there is a connection between lack of a father figure and problems such as delinquency and low academic achievement. Men and employers may need to re-evaluate their roles and responsibilities.

For many men the desire to care for children runs deep. They are often frustrated by the traditional family structure which makes it hard for them to build close relationships with their children. Therefore, they are sharing more of the chores and pleasures of parenthood with their partners. They attend the birth, change diapers, and help at playgroup. Most find this intimacy with their children rewarding and children benefit from a father who is caring and attentive.

Industrial production not only propelled men into high-status occupations; it also gave women paid employment. Nowadays, many urban families cannot meet their material needs with a single income. Globally, women are becoming the majority sex in the workforce and most of the domestic income is often earned by women and children. Paralleling the Western history of the emancipation of women over the past century are signs of a gradual domestication of men. Changes in work and family patterns in recent decades, such as single parenthood and unemployment, have changed traditional sex roles. Men comprise the largest proportion of long-term unemployed. Those who take their role as breadwinner as a major part of their identity may have difficulty adjusting to unemployment and helping with child care and domestic chores.

Husbands may choose to stay at home to care for children if their wives have greater earning power. Few couples have the courage to adopt this life style in practice. In one US study only 4 out of 3600 men cared for their children full-time. Yet many men find they enjoy being full-time fathers and housekeepers. Nowadays, the distribution of authority within the family is less clear than in the past. Increasingly, men and women must negotiate the terms of their partnership.

Sweden is one of the few "father-friendly" countries. Swedish parents may take two months antenatal maternity leave, 10 days paternity leave, and a further 12 months parental leave which is paid to a level just below current income. The couple divide their leave as they wish, although only one parent can take leave at one time. In addition, parents can take time off to care for sick children. To meet the cost Swedes pay more taxes

the caregiving father

Changes in work and family patterns are changing traditional sex roles in many parts of the world. The man is not automatically the family "breadwinner" (left).

Parenthood is uniquely rewarding and challenging. It is also life-changing; adjustments have to be made by both partners. For a father (right), it is an opportunity to express emotions not normally encouraged by society.

than the citizens of almost any other country. Even with such benefits, Swedish men take far less parental leave than women.

Media images of fatherhood have been undergoing a quiet revolution. In a study of the US media it was found that the pre-1970 depiction of men as caregivers was of bumbling, ineffective individuals. Today, this has changed to a potentially effective and important role in the social and emotional development of children. Also in the US, a magazine "Full-Time Dads" is published for caregiving fathers, hoping to end the isolation that fathers who deeply care for their children often face. The joys and pleasures of nurturing small children are a key feature of the magazine. Men who miss out on the nurturing role within a family miss some of the greatest joys in life.

Parenthood

All human societies recognize that when a woman becomes pregnant a new, important kind of relationship develops between her, the father, and the child she will bear. Children are often seen as the physical manifestation of their parents' relationship and as bringing parents closer together. Parenthood can enhance the quality of a couple's relationship, and lead to closer ties with other family members.

Parenthood is physically exhausting, requiring patience, endurance, and commitment. It is also uniquely rewarding and challenging, changing the way adults live and think. Children are a source of great happiness, fascination, and pride, such as when they take their first unsure steps or babble their first words. They have a dramatic impact on the status of the marriage, too. Wedding toasts promise fertility and the personal fulfilment of having children. Before the first child is born the marriage may easily be ended; afterwards, divorce is more difficult. Children ensure their parents' acceptance within their families and within their communities.

"Children ensure their parents' acceptance within their families and communities"

The changes and adjustments parenthood brings are very different for women and men. Pregnancy, birth, and breast-feeding all create a close, physical dependency between mother and child. Except in cases of early abandonment, a child always knows its mother. The family provides a context not only for the child's development, but for the parents' personal growth as well. Motherhood is a powerful part of most women's identity and may be a means of self-validation. For fathers, too, parenthood can give new meaning to life, although there are fewer assumptions about fatherhood, and fewer expectations of them. A man's life is less changed by parenthood than a woman's: he does not endure the physical impact of bearing children; he maintains more social contacts outside the home. Fatherhood, however, allows men to express emotions not otherwise encouraged by society.

In the West, parenthood means hospitals, playgroups, and schools. Children are compared, measured, and examined. Signs of slow development kindle parental concern. Parents become convinced of the need to stimulate their children by exposure to toys, equipment, and play areas. In wealthy nations it is not enough, as it once was, to look after the bodily health and physical needs of children. Parents must also answer for the mental and moral character of their sons and daughters; for the creation of the new identity. In the West there is the general

● A study in the UK in 1979 showed that only 5% of first and second-time fathers did not participate in the care of their one-year-olds. In 1959 the proportion of fathers who provided no help was 70%.

tendency to regard this identity as something encoded in the genes. Many adoptees feel impelled to seek out their biological parents to find out who they really are. This is in stark contrast to many other societies, where parental responsibilities are greatly diluted, such as when children are raised by their parents' kin, or when the entire community shares responsibility. Many cultures are so uninterested in genetic relationships that it is uncertain whether the biological facts of procreation are understood. Australian aborigines and the Trobriand Islanders of the Pacific, for example, traditionally believed that it was spirits which caused pregnancy.

In the developing world, most parents look to their children for security in their old age. Children also provide vital, extra labour, especially in rural economies (right).

"Parenthood is not a static state – it calls for constant adjustments throughout the children's lives"

Fathers and mothers both encourage developments in their children, but they may do so in complementary ways. Studies suggest that father's play is unpredictable, physically-active, and in short bursts, while mother's play is more repetitive, has more verbal stimulation, and is of longer duration.

Personal development is a life-long process. As children grow, they make new demands on their parents which have to be accommodated. Parenthood is not a static state – it calls for constant adjustments throughout the children's lives.

why have children?

When a Japanese mother leaves hospital after giving birth she is presented with a wooden box containing her baby's umbilical cord, carefully preserved and tied with a ribbon. When she dies it is buried with her, showing how central the life of her child is to her own existence. With motherhood, a woman achieves full adult status. In many places, motherhood defines her very reason for being.

To adults childless by choice, having children may seem a self-sacrifice – the sleepless nights, the loss of spontaneity in friendships, and the drudgery of routine. But most parents are possibly quite selfish – they make these short-term sacrifices because they believe there will be long-term gains for all.

Reasons for desiring parenthood differ according to circumstance and culture. In many developing-world societies, having a large family is an eminently rational strategy for survival. Children's labour is a vital part of the family economy. Quite early in life children's labour makes them an asset to, rather than a drain on, family finances. One study in Java, Indonesia, found that as early as the age of seven, a boy assumes responsibility for his family's ducks and chickens. At nine years, he cares for goats and cattle, cuts fodder, and harvests rice. As early as 12 years he may work for a wage. In cities, too, children often earn incomes as servants or by running errands.

Parents look to their children for security. The vast majority of developing-world citizens have no access to insurance or pension plans, or government social security. Without children, one's future in old age would look bleak. Parents can also hope that their child will be the one who gets an education and a city job. Income from one such job can often support a whole family in the countryside.

In wealthier countries, and among the developing world élite, there is less economic and practical motivation for having children, although some parents would expect help from their children when old.

Of course, the value of children to their parents cannot be measured in terms of labour or extra income alone. Parents' political dreams may be realized when children marry into powerful or prestigious families. Parents whose children excel at school or work gain prestige among their friends and family. Children prove adult potency and so enhance self-image; they also bear their parent's name, and perhaps physical and personal characteristics. Adults gain a sense of continuity with the future; that they will be remembered even after death. Among

"Children yoke parents to the past, present, and future"
Japanese proverb

"Children sweeten labours, but they make misfortune more bitter."
Francis Bacon

people who practice ancestral worship, a dead person's spirit cannot rest unless there is an heir to carry out rituals of mourning and remembrance.

For parents the world over, children offer incomparable satisfaction and joy. For the poorest, the role children play in fulfilling these deep human needs cannot be underestimated.

"Pink for a girl, blue for a boy." All over the world parents treat boys and girls differently. The contrasting expectations of parents quickly become absorbed in the children's own behaviour.

boys and girls

The desire for boys often outweighs the desire for girls, especially among high-density rural populations in Asia. In many cultures, sons are especially important since it is they who will care for their parents in old age. They are seen as the mainstay of the family economy, especially where plough cultivation, herding, and irrigation are the key to the food supply. Daughters, by contrast, are soon married off, and therefore provide fewer years of productive labour for their parents.

In many cultures, the value of males is reflected and reinforced by their sole rights to inherited property. The lower status of females is reflected in cultural attitudes: in the Middle East, special celebrations mark the birth of a son, and in rural China, only a son can worship the ancestors.

Parents' choice of boys over girls can lead to female infanticide, such as in China, where the one-child policy was introduced in 1979. The 1990 census found that there were 111 boys for 100 girls under the age of one. Between 500,000 and 600,000 girl infants were missing.

Due to the comparative neglect of girls in some regions, they will be fed less nutritious food, and receive less health care than their brothers. Recent studies in the Middle East, for example, have shown that girls are statistically more likely to be affected by malnutrition, or die from infection, than boys.

Education has been seen as the gateway to equal gender opportunity. In the West schooling for both sexes, with the same curriculum and opportunities for further education, is now established. The battle for equal attention in the classroom, for non-sexist stereotyping, to encourage girls in maths and science subjects, goes on. But in developing countries, of the 300 million children not in school, two-thirds are girls. They are kept at home by parents who see no value in an educated daughter and need her to help with household chores. In Malaysia, Nepal, and Java, girls work up to 75 per cent more hours each day than boys; yet parents think that the boys' work is more valuable. The girls' work is invisible and taken for granted.

Today, many Western parents hope that if they treat their children the same, the girls will grow up with wider horizons, more confidence, and a personal identity which does not include a sense of inferiority. When society examines girls' experiences, children become "genderless" by the use of terms such as "child survival", "child health", and "child labour". Once we look at gender in such categories, we discover that girls are disadvantaged in every society.

From birth, all over the world, parents treat boys and girls differently. Although the Amazon Indian boy is the youngest (opposite, above), he wears the chief's head-dress. In some regions, many parents see no value in an educated daughter, and need her for domestic duties (opposite, left).

The young

The most dangerous moment in the natural course of a person's life is the moment of their birth. Before the advent of modern medicine it was commonplace to lose baby or mother – or both. This still holds true in the world's poorer countries.

Today, half of all newborns in the developing world enter the world in their mother's or grandmother's homes, with the village "grannie" in attendance. She is the traditional midwife and often an expert in her field but if something goes severely

The under-five mortality rate (U5MR) is the number of children who die before their fifth birthday, for every 1000 live births. It is one of the principal indicators used by UNICEF to measure the wellbeing of children, and countries may be grouped into regions of very high, high, medium, and low U5MR (below). For selected countries, the U5MR statistics for 1990 and 1960 are compared.

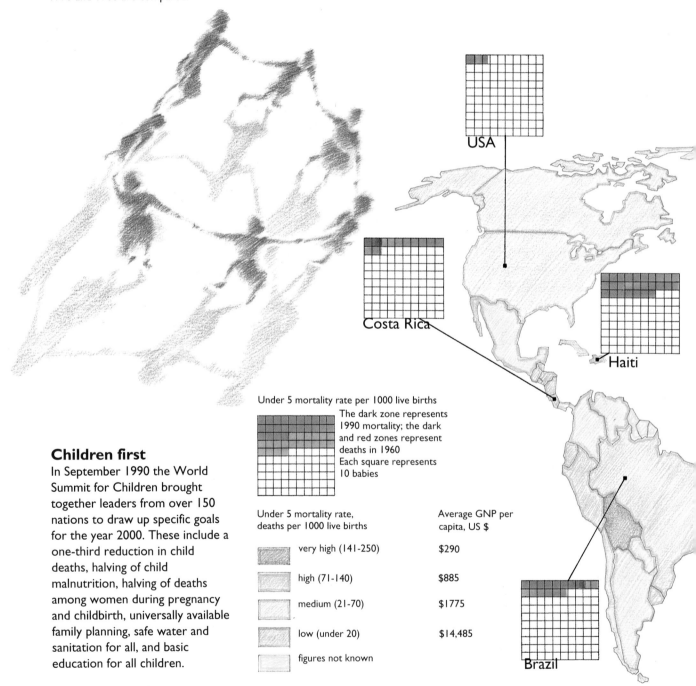

Under 5 mortality rate per 1000 live births
The dark zone represents 1990 mortality; the dark and red zones represent deaths in 1960
Each square represents 10 babies

Under 5 mortality rate, deaths per 1000 live births	Average GNP per capita, US $
very high (141-250)	$290
high (71-140)	$885
medium (21-70)	$1775
low (under 20)	$14,485
figures not known	

Children first

In September 1990 the World Summit for Children brought together leaders from over 150 nations to draw up specific goals for the year 2000. These include a one-third reduction in child deaths, halving of child malnutrition, halving of deaths among women during pregnancy and childbirth, universally available family planning, safe water and sanitation for all, and basic education for all children.

wrong, she cannot resort to life-saving surgery. In the West some women dislike the idea of giving birth in an impersonal hospital environment and opt for a home delivery with a midwife in attendance. They can still summon the emergency services if the need arises.

Once born, a child's chances gradually improve. In the poorest countries, half of the infants who fail to survive to their first birthday die within the first month of life; those with low birth weight are most vulnerable. Each year around 20 million

• Immunization of infants against 4 killer diseases in developing countries rose from under 30% in 1980 to 80% in 1990 (UNICEF).

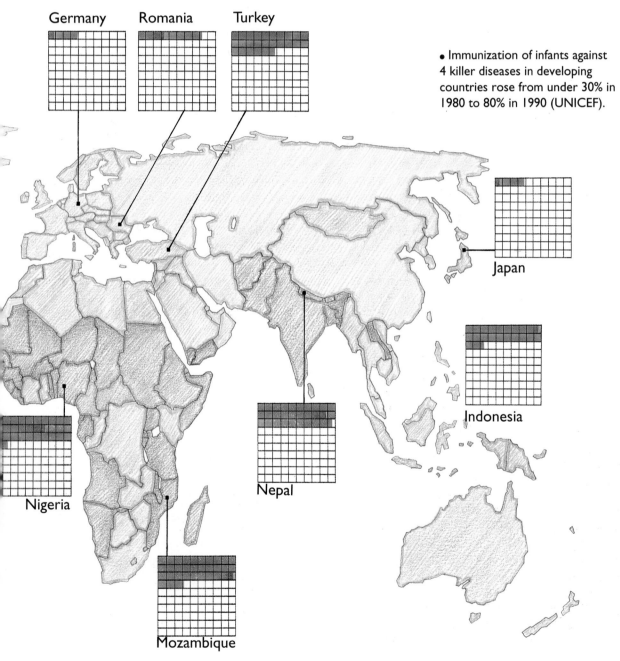

Germany   Romania   Turkey

Japan

Indonesia

Nepal

Nigeria

Mozambique

Fortunate one in eight
A baby girl born in one of the richest countries in 1990 can expect to live to the age of 81. As she grows up she is assured of adequate nutrition, hygenic living conditions, adequate schooling, and advanced medical care. She will spend on average, including government assistance, the equivalent of US $1000 on her health every year.

Deprived one in seven
A baby girl born in the most disadvantaged of the least developed countries in 1990 can expect to live barely 43 years. She has a one in four chance of being underweight, and a high probability of being malnourished throughout childhood. She has a one in five chance of dying before her first birthday and a one in three chance of dying before her fifth birthday. She will have a less than one in four chance of learning to read and write. Her country will spend less than US $1 a year on her health; she cannot afford to pay anything herself.

newborns, out of 130 million worldwide, are born prematurely, or do not grow properly in the womb: the health of the mother and the future wellbeing and development of the infant are intimately linked. Poor nutrition and disease in women, for example, is passed on to infants.

The next landmark, especially in poorer countries, is whether the mother is able to breast-feed. Breast milk passes on a mother's immunity to infection – much needed in an unhygienic setting. Bottle-fed babies, who are often given powdered milk over-diluted with unsafe water in unsterile bottles, are several times more likely to die in infancy. Reversing the decline of breast-feeding in the developing world could save the lives of 1.5 million infants every year, reports UNICEF.

Almost 13 million young children die every year; about four million from diarrhoeal infections, often made worse by poor feeding; and about four million from respiratory infections. Infant mortality has fallen to its lowest global level ever, helped by increased access to immunization, clean water, and sanitation, as well as improved nutrition and the education of women. Twelve out of every thirteen born into the world will live to their first birthday. By the year 2000 the UN estimates this will improve to nineteen out of every twenty.

All children are born with extraordinary potential which can wither, or be supported and enhanced. As a child grows, physically, so he or she develops and learns with an ever-increasing complexity. There has been enormous progress in child survival in recent decades but many of the conditions that once threatened survival now risk impairing a child's early physical, intellectual, social, and emotional development.

In the West, this century has seen much scientific enquiry into child psychology and good parenting. Mothers have abandoned the idea that raising a child is a natural process about which knowledge comes instinctively. It is now accepted that early nurturing influences the emotional balance, self-confidence, and success of the future adult. Every parent daily monitors the young child for signs – rapturously greeted – of new skills. Given the pressures individuals face in the modern world, investment in the development of the young child is a serious business for many parents today.

Such notions, however, may be alien to mothers in poor countries. A baby – usually one of many – is born; the mother

child development

is given "time off" from her regular duties in the weeks surrounding the birth, often staying with her mother or mother-in-law. Then, with the baby on her back, she is again working in the fields, fetching fuel, and carrying water. When the child can walk, he or she will "help" by picking stones from the furrow, or scaring birds away. The investment of time playing with the child and helping skills develop is a haphazard affair.

Evidence clearly shows that a child who is neglected – physically, mentally, or emotionally – will suffer disadvantages which may last a lifetime. A child born with an impairment may avoid permanent disability if given the necessary encouragement and stimulation to develop normally. The family is still regarded as the best environment for a young child's nurture and upbringing, even in disadvantaged circumstances.

Charles Dickens portrayed the impact of the industrial revolution on the children of the English poor; images of small, underfed bodies toiling in the grime of mines and chimneys, and in the stale air of sweatshops and factories. Reaction to the horror

Almost all children are born with a great capacity for learning, which can be crucially affected by the environment in which they develop. This young Ugandan girl (above) practises numbers in the sand at her primary school.

'**I've been working here a long time, since I was a child.**" Ten-year-old Santhanamari (above) works 12 hours a day in a factory in India, packing matches into boxes. "At the end of the day, my fingers are sore and my back aches but I can sometimes earn eight rupees (3 cents). My younger sister is at school but she will leave to come here when there is work available."

of mid-nineteenth century child labour obscured the fact that children had always worked. For centuries, children were born to contribute to, not depend upon, the household.

In developing countries today, in spite of legislation which echoes Victorian reforming attitudes, millions of children spend their days neither at school nor playing, but working.

In India the child workforce – organized and informal – is reckoned to number 44 million. Parents cannot afford to give their children a long period of dependent nurture. City boys are out shining shoes, parking cars, collecting trash, and selling newspapers to help swell family income. Girls from the age of five upwards look after siblings, wash dishes, and prepare food. Many are domestic servants, working around the clock in return for a patch of floor to sleep on and leftovers to eat.

Reformers now recognize that ending child labour at one stroke is impractical in many societies. Instead, they focus on

In India, the child workforce is estimated to number 44 million. They work long hours, frequently in poor conditions. Many are employed in the weaving industry, such as this boy working a silk hand loom (left). Others are employed in potentially dangerous work, such as in match factories (far left).

A UNICEF study in the Philippines shows that three-quarters of street children return to their parents at night, and earn up to a third of family income. Up to 75,000 children roam the streets of the capital, Manila – those under 14 years of age are sometimes rounded up at night (below) before appearing in front of a juvenile court.

children at work

In 1992 seven-year-old Madan Ram was rescued, with two other boys, from slavery as a carpet maker in the village of Nadini, in Uttar Pradesh state, India.

Activists from the South Asian Coalition on Child Servitude carried out a successful raid nearby by posing as wool merchants. When they reached Nadini, the children they were seeking had been taken to a hiding-place. They were released by the loom-owner only after two hours of argument.

Madan's elderly father, Paltan Ram, was there to embrace his emaciated son, a victim of abduction. Madan was one of the luckier ones who are rescued or escape; some are not so fortunate. Five years before, a money-lender persuaded the mother of nine-year-old Mahendra Chowdhury to take out a loan of 50 rupees ($1.50) and, as surety, to hand over her son to be apprenticed to a carpet weaver. Mahendra was taken 100 miles away to work in the "carpet belt", but his brother eventually found him. The money-lender insisted that because the boy's work did not cover the cost of his food the loan had risen to 5000 rupees ($150), a sum the family could not hope to raise.

Campaign groups claim that children make up to 80% of hand-made carpets from the Indian sub-continent. Many work 14-16 hours a day in unventilated, ill-lit conditions, and are beaten if they fail to work fast enough or ask to go home. With sparse food rations and no exercise, they become weak. Their lungs become infected from inhaling fluff.

work of an especially exploitative or dangerous nature, and try to impose age limits, safety regulations, and time off for schooling. A phenomenon attracting increasing attention is the exploitation of young children as prostitutes. Girls as young as seven years old are sold into slavery in Thailand's most notorious tourist industry. Over one million children worldwide are thought to be trafficked, or forced by destitution and abandonment, into selling sexual intimacy.

As well as the dangers associated with children's material value – whether labour or the horrors of vice – young people face many potential dangers as they grow into adolescents. Gang fights and vandalism are familiar companions to adolescents in the West and in many cities in the developing world.

The seemingly inevitable progression from childhood innocence to adolescent defiance fills many parents with dread. US studies indicate that in recent decades, the high school drop-out rate has increased, academic performance has declined, and teenage pregnancy and abortion have risen. Delinquency rates climbed by 130 per cent between 1960 and 1980. Suicides, road accidents, and murders pushed up mortality in the 15-19 age group at a time when mortality for the total population fell.

Everywhere, drug and alcohol abuse are increasing dramatically. Impulsive sexual behaviour and intravenous drug use – most common among teenagers – boosts the risk of HIV and AIDS. The WHO estimates that at least half of all people infected with HIV are under 25 years old. Youth crimes such as picking pockets, shoplifting, burglary, and fraud are often linked to drugs. Globally, young males commit most crimes. Large cities such as New York, São Paulo, and Manila experience a disproportionate amount of juvenile delinquency, especially theft.

Kailesh Satyarthi, chairperson of the South Asian Coalition, gave up a successful career as an engineer to devote himself to the eradication of bonded labour. After a 10-year campaign his India-based organization had succeeded in freeing only 5000 children out of an estimated 300,000 working in the carpet industry. It was decided to launch a campaign overseas where the carpets are sold. The South Asian Coalition argues that until there is a reliable scheme introduced for carpets to be labelled showing that they have been made by adults, there should be a boycott of Indian hand-made carpets.

youth and adolescence

In the rural areas of developing countries, young people have a short childhood out of economic necessity. By the time they are in their early teens most have the responsibilities and behaviour of adulthood. By contrast, Westernized families ban children from the adult world – they go to bed earlier, eat different food, and do not work. They are excluded from major family events such as birth or death and may be prevented from witnessing family rows. The adult world is an alien place – the transition to it is fraught with difficulties.

Before the 1950s, Western families and schools were responsible for socializing the young. Today, as parents seek their own fulfilment, so they give less time to their teenagers. Schooling is prolonged and economic dependence on parents may continue into legal adulthood. Young people find this ambiguous situation frustrating. They are also driven to "make something of themselves", but often with insufficient parental guidance and support. Many teenagers "opt out" of their parents' lifestyle, turning instead to the all-pervasive youth culture, which has spread around the globe.

Millions of India's urban teenagers, for example, are in the sway of a Western-style culture, including pop music, fast food, slang, and Hollywood films. The product of India's 150 million-strong middle class, they are tending to shed traditional constraints and many openly display rebellious attitudes toward middle-class values.

❝ **I was a very unhappy person before I came here. Now things look much better to me. Here I have found a family."** After a night working on the streets of Recife, Brazil, some girls find temporary refuge at the Casa de Passagem. For others it is a home where they are helped to break free of prostitution. It has changed the life of 16-year-old Prazeres: "We don't just benefit from the Casa, we are part of it."

Ana Vasconcelos, the Casa's director, stresses the importance of the girls rebuilding their shattered self-esteem – through the painful process of examining their lives. In discussion groups, the girls share their feelings about childhood experiences and family relationships. Many blame their mothers for their predicament, but gradually come to realize that they may have been too young and lacking in skills to be able to look after a child.

Girls who have no family can live in the Casa's community homes. There they earn a small income from catering and have the support of a substitute family, particularly important for those girls with babies or small children.

Ana is realistic about the extent to which the Casa can help. "If you ask me how many girls really change their thinking in the sense of realizing citizenship, it is very few, but our programme is very young. Last year we had 18 girls who really changed and who are now workers, training and educating younger street girls. But all the girls change a bit. The older ones may never change the society in which they live. But they will behave differently toward their daughters. There is no difference between a girl in Recife and a girl in London. A street girl is just a girl who has nothing."

We are living in a decade where the number of children born each year is reaching its highest ever level – the UN predicts that births will begin to decline early next century. More children survive into adulthood than ever before. The children of this decade are the largest generation ever entrusted to adults.

Despite comprising almost half the human race, people under 18 years of age are often ignored, or not heard, by governments. Until 1989 there was no national or international legally-binding treaty on how the rights of all children could be protected. In that year, after a decade of negotiations, the United Nations General Assembly adopted a Convention on the Rights of the Child. This landmark legal instrument set universal standards for the protection of children against neglect, abuse, and exploitation, as well as supporting their rights to survival and special care in the most vulnerable phase of life.

By 1993, 126 countries had ratified the Convention, and many had begun to change national laws and provisions to bring them in line with the commitment they had made.

The cause of children's wellbeing rarely arouses controversy, but the concept of children's rights is not so straightforward as it appears. A child is by definition a minor; an individual not yet mature enough – physically, intellectually, or psychologically – to have outgrown the need for adult guidance and dependence. The case of Gregory Kingsley, the twelve-year-old who was granted legal permission in 1992 to "divorce" his biological mother and live with his foster parents, put the spotlight on children's rights. In many cultures, the concept of a child asserting him– or herself against parental authority, and gaining sanction at law, is inconceivable.

To those who framed the Convention the idea was not to enfranchise children in a rebellion against adult control, but to ensure that children receive the nurture, care, and guidance they need. There are millions of children around the world denied their right to food, health care, love, and educational opportunity. Some children – such as those violently treated – are suffering gross abuses of rights. The Convention now provides some possibility of redress.

The Convention also enshrines the right of children to express their own views and have these taken into account by those making decisions about them. It marks a formal end to the old adage that "children should be seen and not heard." The child's voice may not dominate, but it will be heard.

The 1989 UN Convention on the Rights of the Child has been hailed as the "Magna Carta" or "Bill of Rights" for children. It is the first international legal code on children's rights and has been ratified by 126 countries. Its overriding aim is that all children should have the right to "survive and develop" to their full potential (right). Spending on defence, however, takes a greater share of government expenditure than education in many countries (below).

Saving the children

UNICEF has estimated that it would cost $25 billion a year to protect the world's children. This would halve the rate of child malnutrition, control childhood diseases, and provide almost every boy and girl with at least a basic education. This sum is equal to ten days global military spending.

50% USA

50% NICARAGUA

50% COSTA RICA

BRAZIL

50%

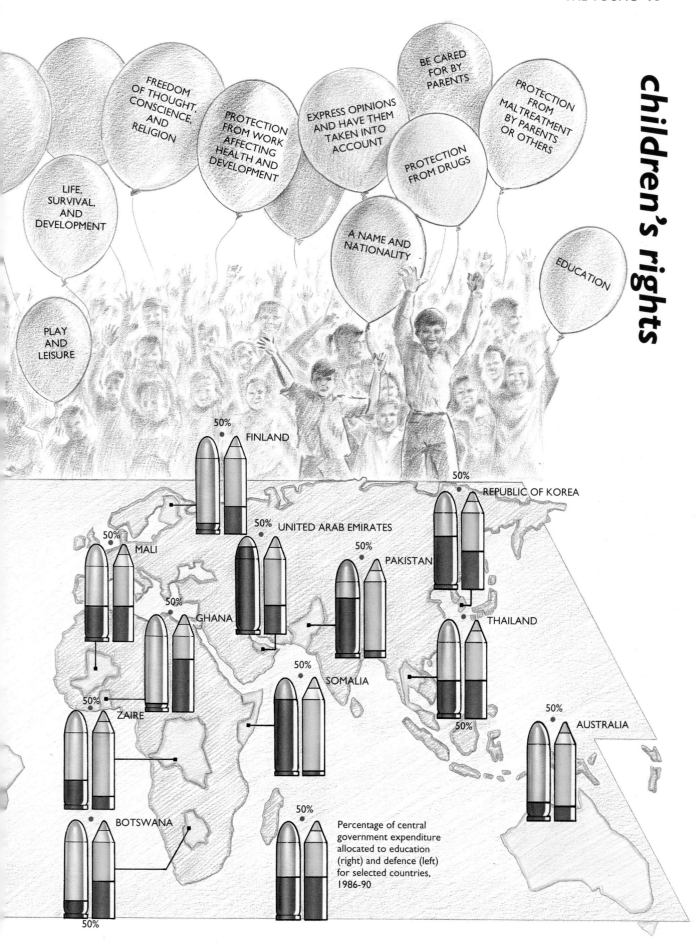

children's rights

FREEDOM OF THOUGHT, CONSCIENCE, AND RELIGION

BE CARED FOR BY PARENTS

PROTECTION FROM WORK AFFECTING HEALTH AND DEVELOPMENT

EXPRESS OPINIONS AND HAVE THEM TAKEN INTO ACCOUNT

PROTECTION FROM MALTREATMENT BY PARENTS OR OTHERS

PROTECTION FROM DRUGS

LIFE, SURVIVAL, AND DEVELOPMENT

A NAME AND NATIONALITY

EDUCATION

PLAY AND LEISURE

50% FINLAND

50% REPUBLIC OF KOREA

50% MALI

50% UNITED ARAB EMIRATES

50% PAKISTAN

50% GHANA

50% SOMALIA

50% THAILAND

50% ZAIRE

50% AUSTRALIA

50%

BOTSWANA

50%

Percentage of central government expenditure allocated to education (right) and defence (left) for selected countries, 1986-90

Marital instability is on the increase all over the world, particularly in areas of poverty, high unemployment, rapid urbanization, and social change. Living under such conditions can put immense strain on a marriage (left).

The UK Children Act (1989) represents a new approach to parental responsibility in divorce cases. The terms "custody" and "access" have been superseded by "residence" and "contact" – to show that the child is not the "property" of any one parent. Instead, parents have joint responsibility, whether they are the "caring" or the "absent" partner. In the majority of cases, parents agree on arrangements for their children and the court will not make an order unless it is specifically required and it is in the child's best interests.

Families Need Fathers (FNF), a UK-based fathers' rights campaign, argues that in disputed cases fathers are still likely to lose out – and children are denied an adequate relationship with their father. They feel the judiciary still sees fathers as remote figures with whom children expect only brief, formal encounters.

Hugh Mills, a teacher and member of FNF, has two daughters: Zoë and Claire, 13 and 12 respectively. They stay with him every other weekend but, although he lives nearby, are forbidden by their mother to drop by or even telephone. Mills applied to the court for a mid-week visit. His ex-wife conceded that Zoë and Claire had a strong desire for more regular contact, but the judge accepted her view that this would be "unsettling".

Families Need Fathers has provoked strong criticism in certain quarters. One lawyer described it as "a menace to women". She added that although past case law has shown a bias toward mothers, this has been due to economic and social realities affecting child care practices within marriage and, perhaps, to a failure by fathers to challenge prevailing work practices. "The courts also prefer to maintain the *status quo* for children, thus the wife who acquires the matrimonial home is able to provide continuity, which is an important factor for the child".

When a woman seeks to limit the contact between father and children, many would argue it is because she knows how her husband behaved before separation. A common response is: "He wasn't interested in them when we were together, so why should he start now?"

In the view of Families Need Fathers, such a comment is too easily applied to all fathers, and good fathers are discriminated against. Hugh Mills is obliged to accept a strictly rationed role as a parent. And yet: "Friends would say how good I was with the kids. I did most of the basic care. All this means is that I've paid a higher penalty."

The troubled family

Fear of losing custody or contact with children, combined with the bitterness and anger of a failed relationship, make separation and divorce one of the most terrible experiences endured by adults. For most, divorce is a last resort – not simply to end a nightmare, but sometimes for survival.

Globally, marital instability is increasing. Once, social norms forced couples to stay together, however unhappy. Today, these social controls are in decline, and it is easier for couples to separate. Sometimes there is a great gulf between the high expectations of marriage and the reality. With the growing economic independence of women in many regions, it is possible for them to consider raising their children alone. Divorce is also common in areas of high unemployment, rapid urbanization, and social change. Divorce does not indicate a loss of belief in marriage – many divorcées remarry – but second and third marriages have even higher incidences of breakdown.

Research suggests that most children would prefer to live in an unhappy home, rather than face a divorce. Often, children's pain at divorce is merely a prelude to the further distress caused by remarriage. "Adults don't have to change parents, lose parents, get extra parents", one step-child said plaintively, "but children who live through their parents' separation and remarriage do".

Parents made miserable by their own problems often behave unwisely toward their children. Some expect their children to take sides, creating a deep emotional conflict for their young. Most tell their children little about the situation. They tell misleading half-truths about a parent's absence, for example, or introduce new partners unconvincingly. Children become adept at looking for clues in what is said or not said, and catching parents unawares with leading questions.

A child is more likely to cope with divorce if there is a continuing relationship with both parents. However, marital breakdown is often followed by moving to a new area, changing jobs, and starting a new family. These developments are often used as a pretext for losing touch with children from a previous marriage. In New Zealand, Sweden, and parts of the US procedures now exist to help families negotiate joint "residence", so that children can retain close links with both parents. In California, where all separating couples with children must consult a conciliator, the number of contested cases in courts has dropped dramatically.

divided families

"Divorce epidemic"
Rising divorce rates in the industrialized North has caused people to fear the demise of the nuclear family. Writing about what she terms the "divorce epidemic" in the US, the analyst Marie Winn says: "The disappearance of marriage as a dependable, permanent structure within which children can live out their childhood is surely the most consequential change that has occurred in the last two decades. Before 1950 divorce was a relatively uncommon occurrence in families with children. By 1982 one out of every two marriages ended in divorce."

the dark side of the family

As a precaution against attack or abduction children are told to avoid deserted alleys or empty playgrounds. They are cautioned not to talk to strangers, or accept gifts from them. These people and places, however, are statistically not such a threat to the young. Most child abuse takes place within the privacy of the family and the home; most assaults and murders are domestic. Nor is child abuse a one-time event, since it tends to continue over extended periods of time.

It is estimated that around four per cent of all children in the US and Western Europe experience serious violence within the home each year. Sexual abuse may be less physically damaging to children, but has a devastating psychological impact – leading to depression and loss of confidence and self-esteem. A survey in Cairo found that up to 45 per cent of families contained girls who had been sexually abused by a relative or close family friend. Emotional abuse, too, may involve isolating, terrorizing, or humiliating a child; neglect may entail the deprivation of food, health care, and love or attention.

Sadly, the home is not always a sanctuary, but a place of fear (above). It is believed that domestic violence against women is the most underreported crime. Physical, sexual, or emotional abuse can seriously affect children, causing depression, loss of confidence, and lack of self-worth (left).

In the majority of countries child abuse and neglect are taboo subjects, and lack of research and statistical information makes it impossible to draw conclusions. Some researchers believe that child abuse is relatively more common where importance is attached to the privacy of the nuclear family and where urbanization and rapid social change have undermined many old family values. By contrast, a low incidence of child abuse is reported for many more traditional cultures.

In places as diverse as lowland South America and Papua New Guinea, infanticide and abandonment may be more common than keeping and abusing children; those that are kept – and survive – are wanted. Where the extended family remains intact, shared parenting – with grandmothers and other female relatives providing relief in child-care – is an important safeguard against harm to children. Extended family life is very public, making it difficult for adults to indulge in abuse.

Globally, most abuse within families is committed by men; most victims are women and children. In most regions there is considerable tolerance of domestic violence against women. This is often expressed in laws that give men the right to chastise their wives physically and may exclude rape within marriage as a criminal offence.

Violence against women takes many forms, from physical attacks to mental assault, including verbal abuse, extreme possessiveness, or harassment. Physical attack is often accompanied by sexual violence. A recent UN survey found that in countries as diverse as Kuwait, Samoa, Uganda, Chile, Poland,

For 10 years Kiranjit Ahluwalia, a UK citizen, suffered systematic violence at the hands of her husband, Dipak. One evening Dipak had beaten her, threatened to kill her, and burnt her face with an iron. Three hours later, while he was asleep in bed, Kiranjit poured petrol over her husband and set him on fire.

At the trial Kiranjit's plea of provocation, which would have reduced the murder charge to manslaughter, was rejected. It was concluded that she had time to think about her actions between finding Dipak asleep and fetching the can of petrol.

Recent cases of women, such as Kiranjit, receiving life sentences for killing their abusers have caused controversy. There are disputes over the definition of provocation, and that murder carries a mandatory sentence.

A few defendants have successfully pleaded provocation despite lapses of time between the last act of abuse and killing their partners. Mitigation seems to be accepted when the defendant is considered to have acted in hot – rather than cold – blood. Kiranjit lost her plea because she appeared calm and deliberate, whereas evidence suggests that she was severely depressed. She describes herself as having been "half dead, an emotionless person".

Women's rights organizations, backed by an increasing number of lawyers, are conducting a twofold campaign: for a less rigid definition of provocation; and for an end to the mandatory life sentence, which takes no account of different levels of culpability.

The provision of services for victims of domestic violence is also a cause for concern. Battered women would not be driven to desperate acts if help was available. In 1992, a report on domestic violence by UK health and social work agencies recommended the provision of a women's helpline, more – and better resourced – emergency refuges, and a national consciousness-raising campaign.

The report pays tribute to overstretched social workers but argues that the needs of abused women may be overlooked in the attempt to reconcile families. It wants to see new domestic violence forums, with representatives from social and probation services, to build structured responses to battered women's needs.

and the US, violence against women is greatly exacerbated by alcohol and drug abuse. The majority of women are targets of violence in their role as wife or lover, but they are also victims as daughters, daughters-in-law, sisters, sisters-in-law, ex-wives, ex-lovers, and mothers.

Since the frequency and intensity of attacks usually escalates with time, the longer a woman is victimized, the more likely she is to be seriously hurt or killed. Crime statistics from Canada show that 60 per cent of all women murdered between 1961 and 1974 were killed within the family. Research from Thailand, Kenya, Bangladesh, and Australia shows similar results. The abuser is also at risk because a significant proportion of women who murder do so in self-defence.

Abuse against women and children is closely linked. Statistics from the US journal Ms show that 53 per cent of men who batter their wives also abuse their children. Children whose mothers are victims are more likely than others to engage in delinquency or to form violent families when they grow up.

Many criminologists believe that domestic violence against women is the most underreported crime. In incest cases especially, victims tend to feel humiliated and shamed, and sometimes guilty. Usually they choose to put up with abuse rather than risk family breakup or social ostracism. Even when women and children do speak up, few people are prepared to listen or take them seriously.

danger in the home

'We go out to rural areas and talk to children and parents, we get children walking in off the street, we get referrals from teachers, doctors, and the Family Court – and I believe this is only the tip of the iceberg."** Gloria Walters, of Jamaica's only Child Guidance Clinic, believes that the incidence of child sexual abuse on the island is higher than the official estimate of one in eight children. A 1989 survey by UNICEF and the Planning Institute of Jamaica found that children under the age of nine were particularly vulnerable.

The first challenge is to get parents – especially mothers – to recognize signs of acute psychological distress. Gloria Walters explains: "Children can be aggressive, depressed, playing truant, afraid of people – particularly men – hyperactive, disobedient, unresponsive, and silent. They might also run away, or lie, steal, and be chronic bedwetters. We educate parents and teachers so they can understand these warning signs when something is not right."

Grace Phillips, a social worker with the Kingston-based Child Care Development Centre, also believes in educating families to tackle the problem. She travels around the poorest areas with her folding table, TV, video, and flip chart, and holds open air meetings. Skilfully, she coaxes children to articulate their feelings about being abused and records their replies on her flipchart, asking the mothers to take note. Then she asks the children to listen while their mothers talk about their problems. This encourages greater understanding and a shared recognition that children have the right to protection from abuse.

grandparents to grandchildren

The aged

Among traditional Muslim families in rural Egypt, women of child-bearing age are veiled and live in seclusion. From puberty they are confined day and night within their home, venturing out only rarely. They have no say in decisions taken by the family. Only the birth of the first grandchild grants Egyptian women the right to be seen and heard.

In many traditional societies today grandparents have an essential role in family life, and are much revered. Grandparents are the transmitters of knowledge, moral values, and life skills to the growing generation. Their experience helps during family crises and in the day-to-day management of family affairs. The grandmother will assist with the birth of her grandchildren and teach them the ancient ways of their culture. The grandfather has more time and patience than the father to teach grandchildren how to hunt, fish, or carry on a craft.

Grandparents are important caretakers of children. In Nigeria, surveys suggest that almost half the children are looked after by grandmothers while their parents work. Many African and Caribbean grandparents raise children alone, while parents work in cities. Caribbean parents often do not help financially, and grandparents have to prolong their working lives by many years. In wealthier regions grandparents are a hidden sector of child care. In the UK, more than a third of mothers who return to work leave their children in the care of grandparents. These women rely more on grandparents for child care than private child-minders, nurseries, and nannies combined.

In rapidly modernizing cultures, the wisdom of the old is less valued; their knowledge deemed unnecessary. Elderly people, once powerful patriarchs and matriarchs, are now frequently considered a burden on the family and society. They are urged to retire; to "make way for the young". Parents turn to experts – family doctors, paediatricians – for guidance on raising their children, rather than to grandparents. The elderly often have little work or educational experience in common with their grandchildren, and the two can sometimes be left with nothing to say to each other.

In the Philippines, 98 per cent of the over-60s live with their families. In many other parts of the world, however, younger people find this arrangement costly and at the expense of their independence. In urban regions especially, the extended family is being abandoned in favour of privacy. A high proportion of elderly people are forced to live alone or in institutions.

The grandparent-grandchild bond is a very special one. Through it, cultural identity and values are passed on and preserved. This Spanish gypsy family (left) emigrated to France 12 years ago, but their culture is passed on to the grandchild.

This enforced isolation and idleness of grandparents is ironic since in many families it occurs just at the time when parents are driven to distraction juggling competing work commitments with child care arrangements.

Throughout the world people are living longer because of improved nutrition, hygiene, and health services. Globally, people over 80 years of age are the fastest growing population group. Sweden has more elderly people in proportion to its total population than any other country. One-fifth of Europe's population is over 60 years, and by 2020 this is expected to increase to more than one-third.

Life expectancy is lower in developing countries, but the annual increase in the number of people over 55 years is currently three times as high as in industrialized nations. This means a marked growth in the absolute numbers of elderly over the next two decades, and an increase in their proportion of the total population.

Western society is becoming generationally top-heavy. In the US there are more grandparents than grandchildren. The ageing of the population has become a major policy issue due to the increase in non-working people relative to workers who fund state welfare schemes. Old people in many Western countries are estimated to cost the state two to three times more than the young. Some Western governments have responded to the growth in numbers of elderly people by concentrating their resources on the over-80s. Younger pensioners are increasingly left to fend for themselves. Even in the wealthy EC, one-fifth of its elderly are living in relative poverty.

The elderly in France
As in the rest of Europe, France is faced with an ageing population. In 1990, for every pensioner, there were 2.3 working people. By 2005, it is estimated that this will fall to less than two workers, and their contributions to the state pension scheme will not be sufficient to maintain current levels of benefits.

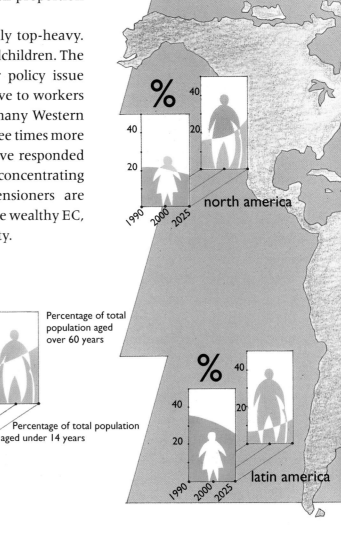

Everywhere, the proportion of the population under 14 years is declining, or set to decline in the early years of the next century. By contrast, the proportion of those over 60 is increasing (right). The industrialized nations, in particular, are becoming generationally top-heavy. The "greying" of the population is now a major policy issue due to the greater health and welfare needs of the elderly. These older people, however, represent an immense resource of experience and ability for both families and society.

Percentage of total population aged over 60 years

Percentage of total population aged under 14 years

north america

latin america

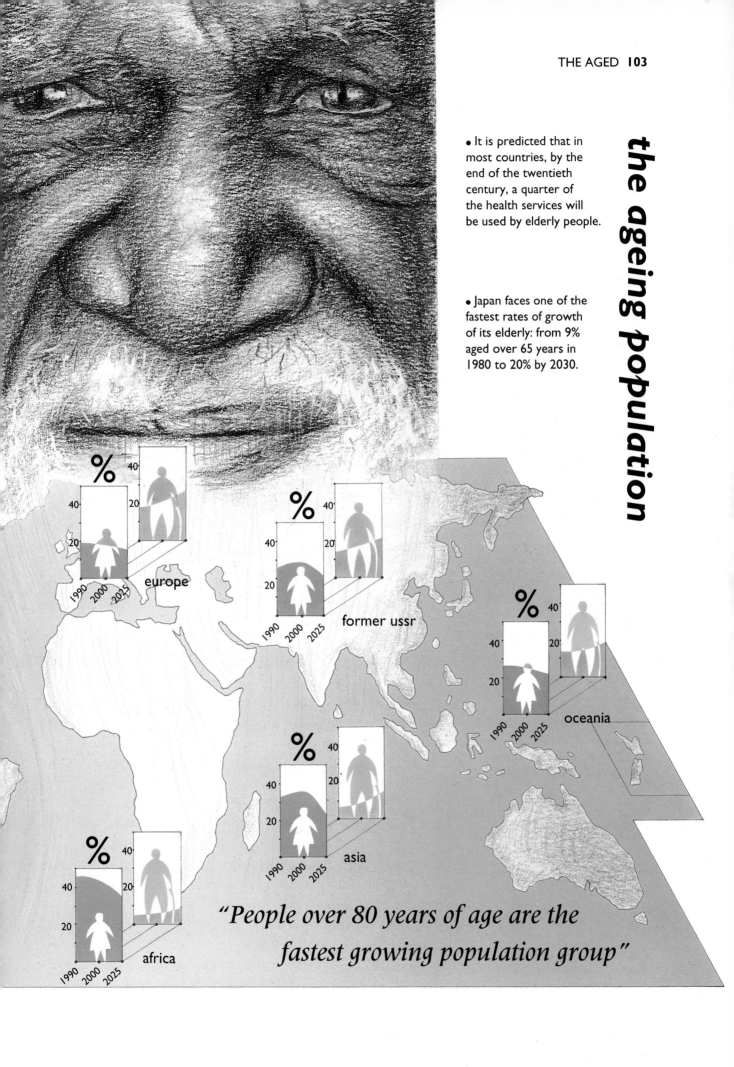

• It is predicted that in most countries, by the end of the twentieth century, a quarter of the health services will be used by elderly people.

• Japan faces one of the fastest rates of growth of its elderly: from 9% aged over 65 years in 1980 to 20% by 2030.

the ageing population

europe

%
40
20

1990 2000 2025

former ussr

%
40
20

1990 2000 2025

oceania

%
40
20

1990 2000 2025

asia

%
40
20

1990 2000 2025

africa

%
40
20

1990 2000 2025

"People over 80 years of age are the fastest growing population group"

In developing countries there are no pensions or other state benefits. Whereas the gap in the life expectancy of males and females is narrowing in industrialized countries, there is a much higher proportion of elderly women in the developing world, particularly among the poorest sectors of the population.

Rent-a-family

Elderly Japanese isolated from their children can now rent a "family" for lunch and a few hours' conversation. They just dial a Toyko number and ask for a daughter, a son-in-law, and two grandchildren, for example. Soon after, the "family" arrives and greets the elderly person emotionally. Three hours with them costs $1130 plus transport.

Among the Samburu people of East Africa men pass through a complicated series of age grades as they grow older – a harmonious process in which their increasing maturity and responsibility are publicly acknowledged. For many people, however, the extra years of life brought by improved health and diet are a mixed blessing. Traditional reverence of the elderly has declined in many parts of the world as a result of technological and social change and new Western values. Conditions for the elderly in modern times can be grim. The media regularly features elderly people mugged on the streets or robbed in their homes. Many old people are afraid to go out.

In mostly rural economies, about 70 per cent of people over 65 years are gainfully employed; the figure for semi-industrialized countries is more than 60 per cent; but in industrialized nations about 20 per cent. In rural societies, elderly people are eased out of the workforce gradually, and the workload within the family is redistributed. In industrialized countries, old age is marked by legally-enforced retirement.

Myths of the greying population still need to be separated from reality. The elderly represent an immense resource. Longer life, early retirement, and better health and wealth than previous generations of the old are redefining family roles.

• In Uganda grandparents are respected, but old people without children or grandchildren are mocked as *nkejje* (dried fish).

The third phase of life – from 65 to 75 – has many possibilities. In Western countries some 70-year-olds may be found studying at university among "peers" half a century younger. In the Netherlands, 80 per cent of the over-65s live independently. But the proportion declines dramatically for the over-75s – life's fourth phase. The proportion of Dutch people of this age living in institutions is one of the highest in the world, although the authorities are experimenting with housing to make it possible for the elderly to live independently. "Kangaroo houses" are one innovation, where an ageing parent lives downstairs and an adult child and family upstairs. "Tandem houses", too, are another experiment, where parent and child live close to each other. Most people find it easier to accept old age if they are healthy and have a role in their family or community.

"Grow old along with me!
The best is yet to be,
the last of life, for which
the first was made"
Robert Browning

the wealth of experience

 **The sharp rise in the size of the elderly population, especially in the industrialized nations, gives huge potential for "grey lobbies" – organizations challenging ageism in society.**

In the US, such organizations are well established. The "Gray Panthers" is a radical action movement formed over two decades ago "to fight age discrimination in public and economic policy and to work for social justice". Most members are in the over-65 age group, but a significant minority consists of younger people; the movement's motto is "age and youth in action". While the campaigning focus is on grey issues, the Panthers also have a much broader social agenda.

Founder Maggie Kuhn explains that far-reaching dreams have always inspired the Panthers and guided their campaigns. "We who are older have nothing to lose. We have everything to gain by living dangerously. We can be risk takers, daring to challenge systems, policies, life styles, ourselves. And we who are young have the most to gain from a new direction and the most to lose without one."

The Panthers have many practical achievements to their credit. They have exposed nursing

Groups to promote the interests of the elderly are appearing everywhere. In Germany a new, radical political party has been formed by retired people – "the Greys" (above).

home abuses, brought about new legislation to control the hearing aid industry, and fought for higher interest rates on savings accounts held by pensioners. They have also succeeded in bringing about a rise in the mandatory retirement age from 65 to 70 years, persuaded television broadcasts of the need for media sensitivity on "age" issues, and developed guidelines for media monitoring.

Campaigning for a national health care system has been a major priority in recent years, and the Panthers continue to work on many other issues, such as homelessness, and the special problems of older women and of elderly people from ethnic minorities. Increasing emphasis is placed on the importance of intergenerational action; what happens globally, nationally, and locally – in defence, environment, ageing, and health care – involves people of all ages.

With support and encouragement, disabled people become integral members of the family and society, such as this thalidomide mother feeding her baby (right).

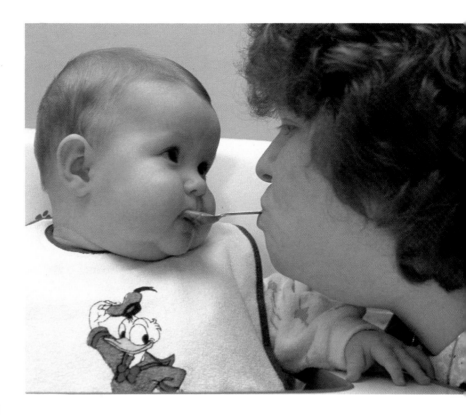

 Six-year-old Pom has Down's Syndrome. He lives with his parents in Klong Toey, one of the poorest quarters of Bangkok. Since birth Pom has needed special attention, but has rarely received it. His parents had to work all day to earn a living and they had no knowledge of special services for disabled children. Pom became withdrawn and unresponsive.

Pom is one of 148 cases of serious disability identified during a house-to-house survey of Klong Toey. The survey, conducted by Save the Children Fund (SCF), found one in three of these children were malnourished, and most parents were labourers with minimal schooling.

A community based rehabilitation (CBR) programme was set up following the survey. Its emphasis is twofold: to help families contribute to their disabled children's development, through enhanced understanding of their needs, and to raise community awareness. Regular visits by a CBR social worker to Pom's family resulted in a strategy to draw on the resources of the extended family. Pom now receives the special attention of 18-year-old Put, a relative who has come from the country to help

Pom, in exchange for her keep and some experience of city life.

Pom's speech, walking, and behaviour have dramatically improved; he is happier and more responsive. He has started to read, with a pair of glasses obtained from a local foundation for mentally disabled children. His status has changed from a "problem" to an integral member of the family.

To change social attitudes is also a crucial part of the CBR approach. In India, Lokesh, a two-year-old boy with cerebral palsy, used to lie in the corner of his parents' one-room house in Bangalore. He was not taught to sit up because a local doctor had told his parents that Lokesh would grow out of his condition by the age of ten.

Through a CBR programme Lokesh's mother, Rajamma, learned physiotherapy to stimulate his movements, and acquired a new attitude which enabled her to

take Lokesh out in a pushchair, ignoring local superstitions that "no one should cast eyes on him".

The aim of CBR has been described as "the empowerment of disabled people and their families to help themselves". Tackling underlying, broader issues is equally important. In developing countries, the major causes of disability are social ones – such as poverty – and development agencies are keen to integrate the disabled into their community work. The other great challenge is to replace fear and prejudice with healthy, positive attitudes; to change our way of thinking about ability, disability, normality, and abnormality.

Disabled people

When a child is born disabled, parents are acutely shocked, and many react with disbelief or anger. Because their child is not strong and healthy in the way they had hoped and expected, they experience a deep sense of loss. Mothers may blame themselves for not taking sufficient care during pregnancy. In some cultures it is believed that misfortune has been visited on the family as retribution for a wrongdoing.

Disability attracts a powerful stigma in most parts of the world, adding a sense of shame and guilt to the many other emotions in the family. In practice, for many disabled people, their physical or mental impairment is far less of a handicap than the ignorance and prejudice of society at large. Disabled people suffer extreme social isolation and powerlessness. Historically in the West – and in many poor countries today – the burden of providing for someone who, it was believed, could not keep themselves led to widespread infanticide. Long-term institutional care was often the only alternative.

The medical profession has, in general, focused on clinical conditions, rehabilitation, and high-cost technological aids. Disabled people all over the world are pointing to social, environmental, and economic factors as the main problem, not medical circumstances. Because of poverty, environmental dangers, war, hazardous housing, poor hygiene, and a lack of health care, there are far more disabled people per head of population in poor countries than rich. One-fifth of all disabilities are caused by malnutrition, and 90 per cent of infant disability is believed to be due to disease and poverty – not genetic in origin.

Care of disabled children is usually left to the family, most often the mother. Industrialized nations usually offer supplementary support in the form of special allowances, therapeutic and rehabilitative services, and respite care for families. Most disabled children in the industrial world receive an education – even if in segregated schools. By contrast, very few disabled children in developing countries go to school, and many die through lack of facilities or support services.

Without support, some families may neglect their disabled members. This not only impedes development, but also damages the confidence of the disabled person, intensifying their dependence on the family and their isolation from the world outside. Families with a more positive attitude build on the person's abilities, give encouragement, and challenge the disabled person.

ability, not disability

Disabled lives

The UN estimates that there are 500 million disabled people in the world. At least 60% of all disabled people – some 300 million – live in developing countries. Only a small proportion of disability is genetic in origin. It is estimated that as much as 85% of adult disability is caused after the age of 13. Malnutrition, physical abuse, industrial accidents, environmental pollution, and stress are other major contributors.

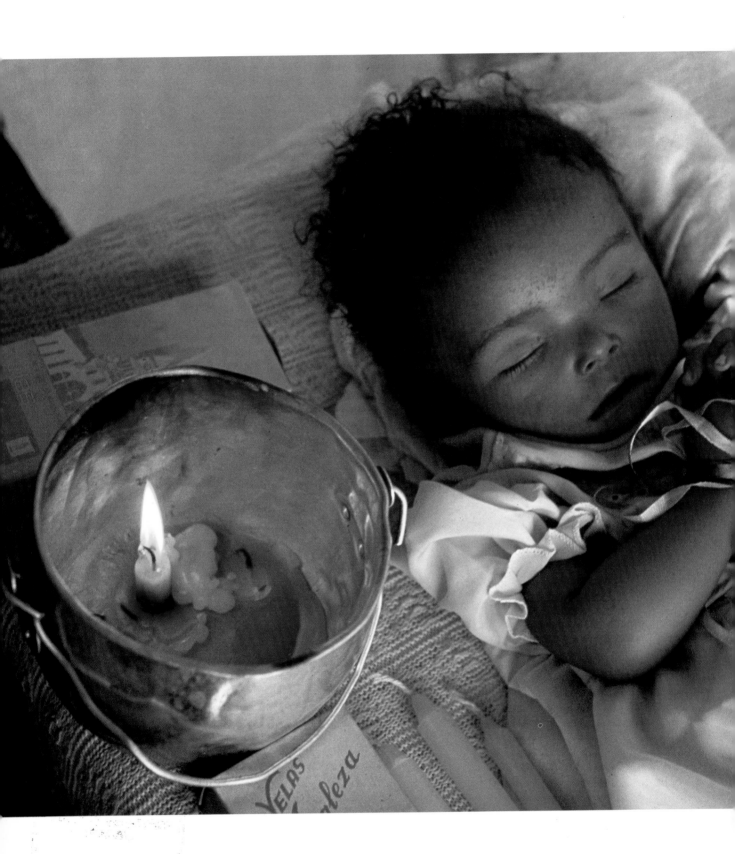

PART FOUR

hostages to fortune

The strength of a nation or a society depends largely on the strength of its families. The relationship between families and society is complicated: what happens in one affects the other. And this section shows how greatly families are being affected by forces outside of their control.

The family which holds together is capable of steering its members through crises. Some families hold together and successfully adapt to the changes. But some are unable to withstand the impact of outside forces. Poverty, wars, environmental decline, AIDS, and economic and social changes in their countries are weakening families. They become less able to protect their members and seek their own solutions. In turn, this can feed the forces acting on them – so much so that the family may fracture.

Global trends are creating difficult decisions for governments and families alike. The wealthiest states, for example, are no longer willing to provide all-encompassing social support. What is the family to do with a member it is no longer able to care for?

The family faces what may be its most difficult challenge in history. Never before have there been so many dramatic social and economic changes in so short a time. The family will almost certainly survive. But what new roles and forms are to come?

Death: in all cultures, ritual surrounds the passing of life. This young baby (left) has accidently died during a pilgrimage in Brazil.

Families and the state

In industrialized countries, the state – the machinery of government – appears to be everywhere, regulating people's lives from birth registration to death certification. Whether it is road-building or industry, food subsidies or taxation, housing or employment, most government decisions and actions have an impact on how families form, how well they function as nurturers and providers, and even on their survival.

Government social policy grows hand in hand with industrialization and urbanization. In the West the change from a family-based rural economy to large-scale industrial

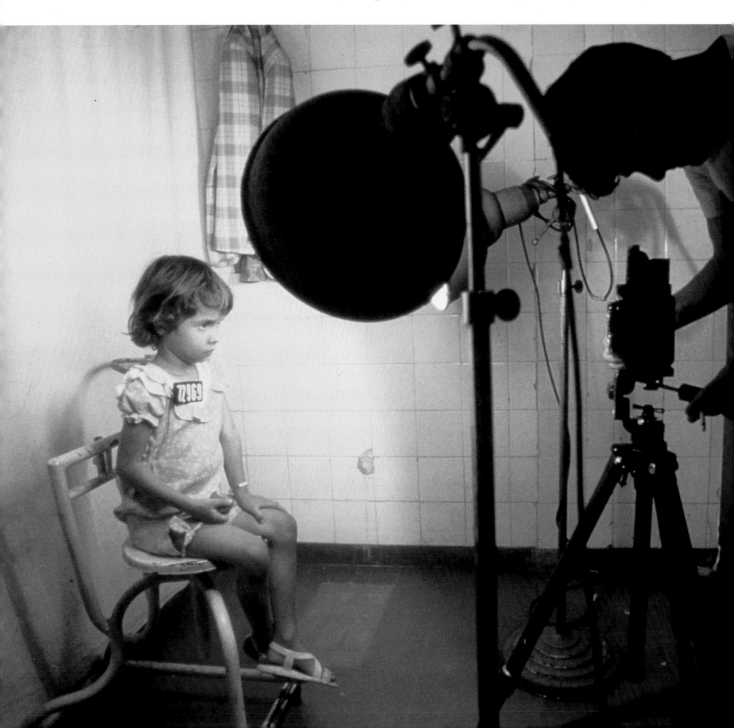

production in the nineteenth century was enormously disruptive to society and to people's daily lives. In pre-industrial society the family was a principal means of ordering social and political life. With industrialization the state assumed many responsibilities that once had belonged to the family, such as care for the poor and dependant. By the beginning of the twentieth century most advanced states had expanded to regulate trade, consumer protection, and wages. Measures to protect health and housing also developed. Most importantly, child labour was abolished, and laws protecting women's interests and universal schooling were introduced.

rise of the state

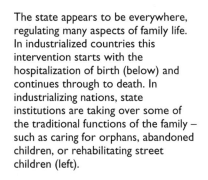

The state appears to be everywhere, regulating many aspects of family life. In industrialized countries this intervention starts with the hospitalization of birth (below) and continues through to death. In industrializing nations, state institutions are taking over some of the traditional functions of the family – such as caring for orphans, abandoned children, or rehabilitating street children (left).

State-run institutions for the sick, orphaned, or delinquent supplement or replace the family's role in many regions. In developing countries, such state resources are often stretched to their limit.

Kenya's urban population tripled between 1980 and 1990, swelled by migrants from rural areas. The shanty towns that have grown on the outskirts of Nairobi and Mombasa, Kenya's second city, bear all the hallmarks of urban poverty. Dwellings are made of cardboard and plastic sheeting, and there is extreme overcrowding and minimal sanitation. There are high rates of separation and divorce, abandonment of women, children working and living on the streets, child prostitution, delinquency, and illiteracy.

Many children run away from home to set up alternative "families" with other street children. In 1988 special Task Forces, supported by UNICEF, were set up in Kenya's principle cities to study the situation of children "in especially difficult circumstances". They have examined the response of the authorities to such children, particularly the limitations of institutions. Kenyan law provides for the protection and discipline of children and young people. Street children can be rounded up and handed back to their parents; if the parents cannot provide protection and discipline their children are placed in an approved school. However, the few institutions that exist cannot cope with the growing numbers of

juveniles being placed in their care and often have to release them back on to the streets.

Nancy Nyawira came to Kirigiti, Kenya's only approved school for girls, at the age of 15; she had been raped by her father. The rape and the subsequent trial traumatized the family; Nancy's mother had a mental breakdown and her children were sent to institutions. Nancy performed badly in her Kenyan Certificate examinations and although she now receives vocational training it will not be easy for her to find a job when released.

Kirigiti houses about 50 more girls than it was built for. Many, like Nancy, are children with no criminal record who have

nowhere else to go; they are orphans or their families are too poor to support them. Living in an approved school exposes them to harmful influences. However, those children who have committed crimes – stealing, fighting, prostitution, selling drugs – also need economic solutions to their problems and help to become part of their community.

The Nairobi Task Force is encouraging institutions to work with parents and also supports the initiatives of voluntary organizations working with children. These are most effective when they strengthen the community's own development efforts, so that it can support its children.

The family acquired a new definition as a private institution – one in partnership with the state. Today specialized agencies complement the traditional roles and functions of the family. In the West, before the nineteenth century, for example, children were socialized and trained in the home – or someone else's – as a servant or apprentice. With the development of an educational system this function was divided: the family became responsible for the early socialization; the school for developing specific skills for work and public life.

Fortunately, in most developed countries, the majority of people have access to some form of safety net of financial support and care if in need – the modern welfare state. Family and child allowances, sickness, disability, and unemployment insurance, and tax breaks are some of the schemes available.

In the face of harsh economic realities, however, governments are retreating from a leading role in providing social services and are returning that responsibility to families. The move toward emptying institutions of, mentally-disabled people and replacing this care with community-based services is one example of how families are being entrusted with these responsibilities. For many reasons, however, families are not always able or ready to take them on.

Most developing countries do not have the funds for widespread state support measures. Where high birth rates, early mortality, and educational wastage are pressing problems, family planning, health, and education services take priority over family welfare policies. In fact the governments of developing countries spend, on average, about one-quarter of their budgets on health and education although the poor majority probably only benefit from half of this. Frequently official records underestimate the rate of marital breakdown and child or wife abandonment, making them a low priority. Many states are also reluctant to intervene in family life, particularly in the Middle East and Africa.

Reconciling the needs and responsibilities of families with those of the state reflects another balance that must be struck: the balance between the rights of individuals and the rights of the family as a whole. Courts, schools, and other state agencies have largely taken from family members the authority to decide what is normal or deviant in family life. Yet while extolling the virtues of traditional family life Western governments are, paradoxically, making it easier to live outside the nuclear family.

Some believe the rise in non-traditional families is encouraged by liberal divorce laws, less punitive treatment of single-parent families, and greater tolerance of cohabitation. The prevalence of state support is even sometimes thought to encourage a teenage girl to become pregnant because she then automatically qualifies for state benefits and a home.

A tendency to identify family failure as the main cause of social problems means some states intervene in family life. One example of extreme action by the social services took place in the UK in 1987, when almost 200 Cleveland children were removed from their homes following allegations of sexual abuse. Chaos reigned as people were falsely accused, and children who had never been abused were taken from their parents. One father suffered a heart attack and a mother decided to have an abortion rather than risk having another child taken away.

Reconciling the state's duty to protect the rights of the individual with the family's right to privacy is, therefore, controversial. There is fierce debate about the identification and treatment of family problems. Who sets the standards families are expected to adhere to, and how do you measure whether families attain them? Even when it is clear that something is wrong, finding a solution is not easy. Many people think, for instance, that removing an abused child from its home is punishing the victim and not the perpetrator.

The state steps in
Most states are empowered to intervene in family life. In the UK, for example, where a child is suspected of being at risk of abuse or neglect, he or she can be taken into care following a court order. Alternatively, parents may voluntarily agree to place their child in care if they cannot cope. In 1990, about 33,000 UK children were admitted to care – more than half were placed with foster parents. Since 1980 the number of children in care has declined by one-third.

Poverty, unemployment, and debt can all severely affect a family's fortunes. Families may be forced to split up to look for work, or may lose their home and be forced to live in unsuitable conditions – even in the family car (left).

Twelve million children in the US, the world's wealthiest nation, are living below the poverty line. Overall poverty, especially among the elderly, has declined in recent decades while child poverty has risen. In the 1950s the proportion of children living in poverty was 27%; in the 1960s this was halved to 14%. Since then it has steadily increased; in the 1980s, a decade of unparalleled economic growth, it rose to 22%.

In America's inner cities 45% of black children and 39% of Hispanic children are officially poor. The Martin Luther King General Hospital in Los Angeles, where most patients are black, saw infant mortality climb from 12 per thousand in 1983 to 18 per thousand by 1990. In 1981, only one mother in ten received no pre-natal care; by 1990 it was one mother in three.

These statistics reflect a bleak reality: the structures of urban life are collapsing under the pressures of drugs, unemployment, street crime, and deepening poverty.

Poverty also exists elsewhere. A report by the Washington-based Children's Defense Fund (CDF) shows that many poor children live outside the big cities, are white, and belong to families with only one or two children.

The CDF attributes the rise in child poverty to reduced government support for poor families with children, and the steady fall in wages (in real terms) for unskilled workers - a 20% drop between 1973 and 1990. The real value of the government-funded Aid for Families with Dependent Children has dropped by 40% in the last two decades. Far from achieving a fair, minimum "family wage", a family with only one child is left $2000 per annum below the poverty line.

In contrast, social security and Medicare have greatly improved the economic situation of the elderly; the proportion of over-65s living in poverty has fallen by two-thirds since the 1960s. Older citizens now make up only 10% of America's poor, while children account for 40%.

"I have begun to regard the growing neglect and poverty of the young as the biggest single threat to this nation's future", says Dr Berry Brazelton, a paediatrician at Harvard Medical School. "I also see evidence that we could start preventing this terrible waste, with remedies available right now – but we seem to have lost the will even to think about it."

The CDF also argues that "our high poverty rate is interfering with the healthy development and education of millions of our children and threatens the nation's economic and social future." It sees the elimination of child poverty as essential to "tackling the educational, health, substance abuse, crime, and other problems that seem so daunting".

For richer, for poorer

In the Chewa language of modern Malawi, the word for "poor" – umphawi – implies a lack of kin and friends. In most of sub-Saharan Africa to be without family is to be destitute.

In fact, millions of families around the world live in such a state, marginalized or excluded, socially, culturally, and economically. In almost all societies, poverty threatens the family's ability to cater for the needs of its members. Although traditionally measured by income, the true horror of poverty extends into all aspects of family life: susceptibility to disease, life expectancy, diet, shelter, and education. Babies born to poor Colombian families, for example, are twice as likely to die in their first few years than the children of richer families. Poverty also breeds powerlessness. Poor families have little or no control over resources such as land, and little opportunity to use their capabilities to better their lives. Development agencies estimate that at least 13 per cent of rural households in the developing world are landless.

The African family, in particular, is under great pressure. Average per-capita income fell by a quarter in the 1980s. Between 1979 and 1985 the number of Africans living below the poverty line increased by almost two-thirds. Per capita incomes have also declined in Latin America and parts of Asia, swamping improvements in other areas such as China. But in Africa environmental degradation, increasing population, and food insecurity have combined to undermine the family's ability to cope – a situation made worse by national debt and world recession.

"There are but two families in the world, as my grandmother used to say, the Haves and the Have-nots."
Cervantes (1547-1616)

In the 1950s and 60s governments in developing countries embarked on the road to industrialization. Ambitious plans were laid to develop export production with the aid of large-scale irrigation projects, hydro-electric plants, and other schemes using foreign technologies. Low interest rates on international money markets, made possible by oil wealth, encouraged developing world governments to finance this by massive borrowing. The first oil shock of 1973 sent oil prices rocketing; borrowing became expensive, and prices for primary exports fell.

Developing countries are now saddled with a seemingly immovable weight of debt – by 1990 some $1300 billion was owed to industrialized governments, banks, and financial institutions. Developing world governments allocate 15 per cent of their expenditure to the servicing of debts. In sub-Saharan

Marriage and recession
In its 1992 annual report Relate, the UK marriage guidance group, stated that unemployment, redundancy, home repossessions, and mounting debts have a "devastating" effect on family life. Between 1987 and 1992 Relate's work load increased by 50% to 70,000 couples.

Reverse aid

The total debt of developing nations has multiplied thirteenfold in the last 20 years. The servicing of this debt means that, from 1983-89, rich creditor nations and financial institutions received a staggering $242 billion in net transfers from indebted developing countries (right).

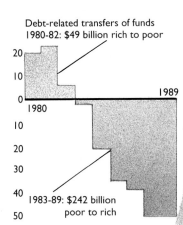

Debt-related transfers of funds
1980-82: $49 billion rich to poor

1983-89: $242 billion poor to rich

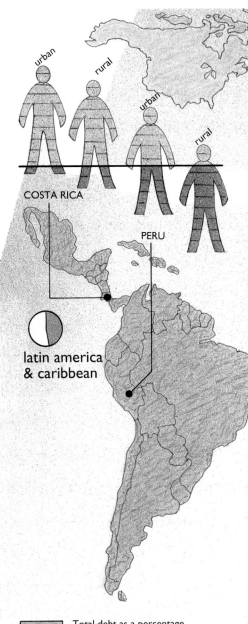

latin america & caribbean

COSTA RICA

PERU

Total debt as a percentage of GNP, for 5 regions and 1 country, 1989

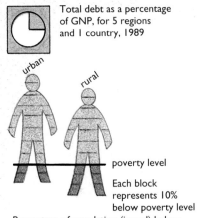

poverty level

Each block represents 10% below poverty level

Percentage of population (in red) below absolute poverty levels, 1980-89

Africa it accounts for one-fifth of all government spending: more than health and education expenditure combined.

The 1980s saw a dramatic downturn in the fortunes of developing countries. Overburdened with this debt and military expenditures, and faced with a sharp fall in export revenues, they were forced to restructure their economies and adopt austerity programmes. Poor families were hit by cuts in essential services such as health and education, and the removal of food subsidies. Unemployment increased and the cost of living rose. Some of the most indebted countries were in Latin America. In Peru and Bolivia, real wages fell by half during the 1980s.

Globally, women suffer most from declining incomes and services, and the withdrawal of food subsidies. In many parts of the developing world they are responsible for providing food, health care, and clothing for children, and also stand in when men are made redundant. They are forced to take on extra paid work to feed the family, yet they cannot give up their domestic duties. Recession has also driven many children out of full time schooling and into the job market early; over 30 per cent of school-age urban children in poor Latin American communities work. In some African and Latin American countries mid-century improvements in child mortality rates are being reversed.

When a family's income is severely depleted, survival involves ruthless decisions. This can mean sacrificing individual welfare for the sake of the family group. In Asia, children are sometimes even sold into prostitution or factory work to pay off

debt and recession

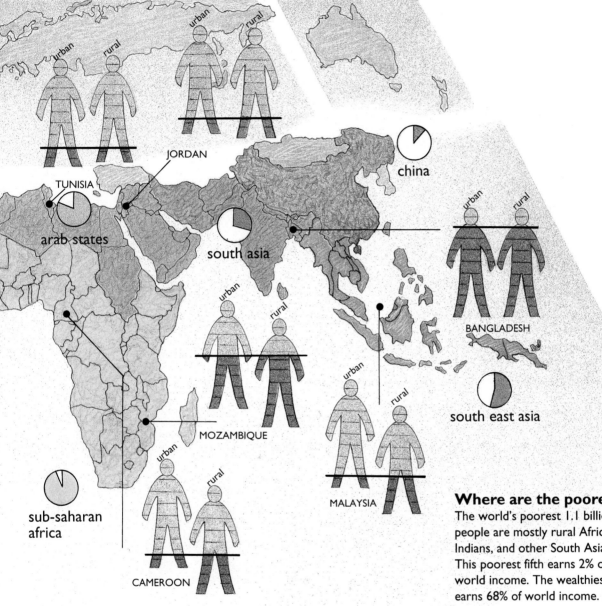

JORDAN

TUNISIA

arab states

china

south asia

BANGLADESH

urban rural

MOZAMBIQUE

south east asia

urban rural

MALAYSIA

sub-saharan
africa

CAMEROON

Where are the poorest?

The world's poorest 1.1 billion people are mostly rural Africans, Indians, and other South Asians. This poorest fifth earns 2% of world income. The wealthiest fifth earns 68% of world income. Even in the UK and the US about a quarter of all children live below the "relative" poverty line.

It is believed that more than one billion people in the developing world live in "absolute" poverty, defined as the income level below which it is impossible to afford basic necessities, such as a nutritionally adequate diet. The map (above) shows the percentage in urban and rural areas of selected developing countries that live below the poverty line. In general, a higher proportion of people live in poverty in rural areas than in cities.

Percentage of population (in red) below relative poverty level

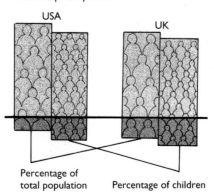

USA

UK

Percentage of
total population

Percentage of children

One day in December 1991 thousands of street children descended on Rio de Janeiro's business sector. Most were under 11 years of age; some looked sad; all had eyes hardened by the daily struggle for survival. Their T-shirts bore slogans proclaiming the right to justice, dignity, education, to be treated as citizens – and the right to life. This was the first demonstration of Brazil's street children against the violence they face in the overcrowded city.

Brazil has the highest number of street children in the world; an estimated seven million. Beatings, persecution, rape, and murder are commonplace. An Amnesty International report revealed that at least one child a day is killed by death squads, with undisputed police complicity.

There is hostility towards the children – even an unspoken tolerance of the assassins – among the general public. Street kids are deemed nuisances and criminals, although only a minority engage in criminal activity. Most are simply trying to scratch a living by cleaning windscreens, shoe-shining, selling articles made from scrap, and begging.

The children on the march wanted to impress on Brazil's more fortunate citizens that they are human beings, forced on to the streets out of necessity. In many cases they have to fend for themselves when their mothers, for want of other employment, take live-in jobs as domestic servants. Often, contact with family breaks down completely. Mothers of "disappeared" children are left not knowing if they are alive or dead.

It started with a few families without any organization," remembers Ruben, one of the first settlers of an Argentinian squatter town. "On the following days more people arrived, some of them when they saw the crowd, others as soon as they got to know through the newspapers. At first it was very hard. I lived under an umbrella for two months."

On 22 January 1986 in Matanzas, a district on the outskirts of Buenos Aires, a dump site began to give way to an urban settlement which now houses some 3000 families.

"We had to get organized in order to survive," explains Ruben. "We allotted plots of land, marked out blocks for each group of 24 families, appointed a representative for every 20 or 30 families, and set up soup kitchens. We found that blocks of 60 metres were more appropriate, since we wanted to avoid the misuse of land. We drew up the designs in such a way that nobody had to occupy the lowland, which is easily flooded."

Vagrancy is an offence in most countries and homeless people have no – or few – rights, making them vulnerable to maltreatment and exploitation. These street children in Brazil (below) are demonstrating for the right to be treated as citizens.

housing and homelessness

debts. Child labour can tighten the vicious circle of poverty. In areas with high adult unemployment, the number of children at work is the greatest.

The uneven distribution of land and resources in many parts of the world forces the poor to live in unsafe areas. Countless rural families live on land prone to desertification, drought, cyclones, flooding, or bush fires. Impoverishment drives millions into the cities, where families may face the hazards of life in the slums, shanty towns, and on the streets.

With high real estate prices and most land ownership concentrated in the hands of a few, poor urban families have little hope of obtaining land or housing legally. In greater Bombay, for example, one particular family owns 2000 hectares of vacant land – enough to house most of the city's slum and pavement dwellers. In such cities thousands sleep in the open or build dwellings from sacking and poles. Huge numbers come from rural areas, pulled by the greater city opportunities, and pushed by land seizures, debt, or the loss of the principal wage earner.

Vulnerable family members are the ones most likely to be homeless, particularly in times of social upheaval. In Russia, in the early days of the Revolution, hundreds of homeless youngsters lived by stealing and begging, and several hundred thousand juvenile "hobos" roamed the highways and railroads of the US during the depression of the 1930s. Today in the West, many people leave home for personal reasons: young people run away from abuse or neglect; adults leave because of relationship breakdown, made worse by job loss or drinking problems.

"70-95 per cent of new housing in most developing world cities is unauthorized"

Because the poor cannot afford formal housing or meet the legal requirements of ownership, they find informal, creative ways of obtaining shelter. Throughout dozens of developing world cities, poor families are determining the direction of urban growth. In cities as diverse as Bangkok, Bombay, and Bogotá, more than one million people live in squatter settlements or shanty towns on illegally-occupied land. An estimated 70-95 per cent of new housing in most developing world cities is unauthorized. In the Peruvian capital Lima, for example, the

● The worldwide total of homeless people is estimated at 100 million (Worldwatch).

Hong Kong housing
The mid twentieth century saw an influx of refugees from China to Hong Kong. Crowded tenement buildings were subdivided into cubicles and bed spaces; flat roofs were also let and many families even slept on pavements. The 1961 Hong Kong Census recorded other living spaces such as staircases, passageways, hawker stalls, caves, tunnels, and even sewers. Residential density in parts of central Hong Kong was as high as 4000 people per hectare in 1976, the highest ratio of low-income families per hectare in the world.

In the Romanian town of Copsa Mica, fields, trees, houses, and children alike are coated in soot (left). Twenty years ago, the Communist government decided to build a massive petroleum processing and lead smelting plant in this Transylvanian town. The post-revolution government has promised to install filters and other equipment to clean up the plant.

Mozambican border, organized a campaign against the authorities' practice of releasing water from the Jozini dam, ruining crops in the fields. The authorities eventually agreed to consult with community-based "water committees" about the most suitable time and duration for dam discharges, allowing families to live without the constant fear of loss of livelihood.

In Sekhukhuneland, part of the Lebowa homeland, initiatives for sustainable development are under way. The Ikageng Dichweung Women's Association, for example, began with a programme to plant fruit trees and is now planning larger-scale afforestation. This is vital to environmental recovery, as a member explains: "The greater parts of Sekhukhuneland are torn apart by ever deepening dongas (erosion gullies). In years to come we will need bridges to cross over them unless we stop the dongas forming. Our plans include setting up a nursery and tree-planting. The youth, our children, will play a central role in this attempt."

'**The great red hills stand desolate, and the earth has torn away like flesh.** The lightning flashes over them, and the clouds pour down upon them, the dead streams come to life, full of the red blood of the earth. Down in the valleys women scratch the soil that is left, and the maize hardly reaches the height of a man."

South Africa provides an extreme example of the link between environmental destruction and the exploitation of families and communities.

Apartheid forcibly removed vast numbers of people to fragments of territory unable to sustain them. Intense cultivation and over-grazing in these new "homelands" resulted in massive erosion. Now families and communities are working to improve their environment and living conditions. Previously, the black majority had associated the environmental movement with authoritarian policies to conserve wildlife at the expense of people.

In the mid-1980s inhabitants of the Pongola flood plain, near the

value of illegal housing built between 1960 and 1984 was more than $8.3 billion – almost 50 times the amount spent by the state on housing for the poor.

Wherever they live, all families and children are at risk from environmental decline. The water we drink, the food we eat, and the air we breathe are all susceptible. The poor and vulnerable are usually most at risk.

Worldwide it appears that short-term profit prevails over environmental sustainability. Since 1950 the world economy has grown fivefold while human population has doubled. Such growth has begun to outstrip the Earth's capacity to carry this level of activity, and absorb waste without being damaged. The demands for crops and the products of forests, grasslands, and fisheries are exceeding the sustainable yield of these environments. Overstocking grassland with livestock, overfishing, and overcutting forests are now commonplace.

Every country is paying a price for environmental degradation. The industrial countries, with 85 per cent of world economic activity and 23 per cent of its population, account for the majority of mineral and fossil-fuel consumption. One issue alone – the increase of gases in the atmosphere enhancing the "greenhouse effect" – has the potential for altering global climate with significant consequences for everyone – rich and poor.

In the developing countries resource consumption per person is far lower, but the growing population and economic pressures are increasingly damaging local environments. Some 60 per cent of the world's poorest people live in ecologically vulnerable areas. The landless families of Amazonia, for example, are often pushed from marginal environments into even more fragile ones. There, land belongs to a few, leaving the majority with small plots unsuited to continuous production. After cutting or burning areas of forest, the soil loses its fertility and eventually becomes wasteland.

Some experts predict that only concerted international action can avert global catastrophe. Yet the political will for action may be lacking. At the community level, however, thousands of initiatives are making a difference. In the US and Europe, for example, the Global Action Plan (GAP) helps families, friends, and neighbours to reduce their household energy and resource consumption. On the other side of the world in the Indian state of Orissa, the "Friends of the Trees and Living

environmental decline

Growth versus health

The head of the Russian Academy of Medical Sciences said in 1992, "We have already doomed ourselves for the next 25 years. The next generation is entering adult life unhealthy. The Soviet economy was developed at the expense of the population's health." The Academy's data shows that: 11% of Russian infants suffer birth defects; half the drinking water is contaminated, 55% of school-age children suffer health problems (Financial Times).

● One-fifth of the world's population is exposed to damaging air pollution (WHO).

● The US Conservation Reserve Program has cut soil erosion by one-third between 1985 and 1990 (US government).

Beings" was formed by a small group of poor villagers to stop the deforestation of their hills. They persuaded their own village, and then neighbouring settlements, to reforest the area. Environmental education has also played an important part, with families creating tree nurseries and hillside planting. The movement has now reached 1800 villages and been awarded a prestigious UNEP "Global 500" award.

The fractured family

War has changed. At one time civilians were relatively safe and removed from war zones. Today they are frequently the target. At the turn of this century only five per cent of casualties were civilian; but in the Second World War the figure rose to 65 per cent. Now nine out of ten victims of war are civilians. And while there has not been a world war since 1945, there has not been a single day without conflict.

Quite apart from the deaths and injuries that result, war causes suffering in many other ways. In civil wars, normal family and community life ceases as homes and livelihoods are destroyed, inflation rises, and corruption and looting become widespread. Schools and clinics are closed, food and water shortages are common, malnutrition and disease become rampant.

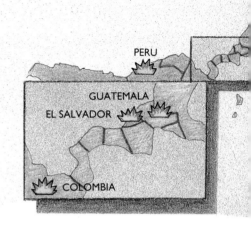

• In the 1950s, the average number of wars was 9 a year; in the 1980s it was 16 a year.

"Nine out of ten victims of war are civilians"

Old people, children, pregnant women, and mothers nursing infants are the most vulnerable in war. UNICEF estimates that in the last decade 1.5 million children have been killed, more than four million physically disabled, and 12 million have lost their homes. During fighting or evacuation families are often separated and children orphaned. Normal family roles are reversed as sick or injured adults become dependant on their children. Sexual violence against women and children is also widespread. Some 20,000 Muslim women and young girls are believed to have been raped by Serbian soldiers in Bosnia in a systematic effort to defile women, jeopardize their future as spouses, and produce Serbian babies.

The emotional effects of armed conflict are often the most difficult to gauge. People who have witnessed violence may experience invasive memories of the scene. Bed-wetting, nightmares, loss of concentration, and learning difficulties are common in children. UNICEF estimates that 10 million children worldwide suffer psychological trauma from wars.

Wars still rage on. The map (above) shows major wars in the early 1990s leading to at least 1000 deaths per year. Since 1945 some 22 million lives have been lost in war. Around half of this total has been in the Far East. Most wars are civil wars. Most lives lost are civilian lives (see graph). Producing and selling weapons is the world's second biggest industry, after oil.

casualties of war

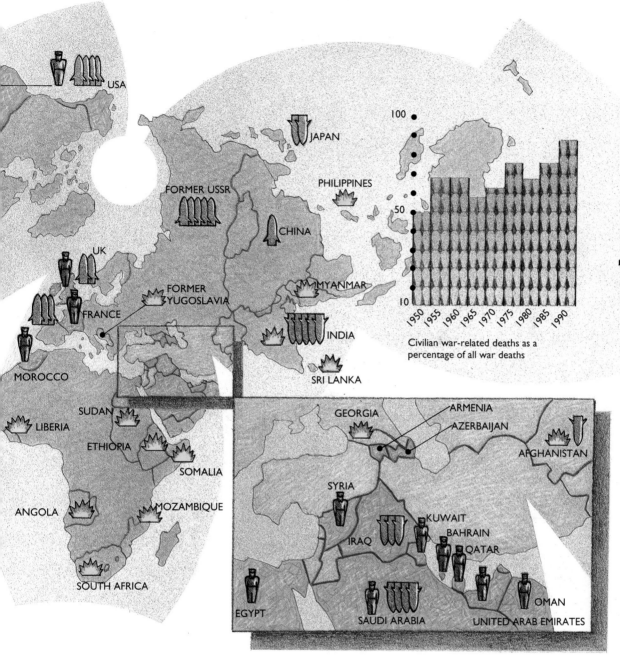

Civilian war-related deaths as a percentage of all war deaths

Major conflicts January 1991–January 1993 (organized armed conflict leading to at least 1000 deaths per year)

Countries with civil wars

Countries at war with other nations

Countries which committed troops to the coalition against Iraq, 1991

Top 5 exporters of major arms, 1987–1991

Former USSR $61,339 million

USA $59,957 million

France $11,220 million

UK $9097 million

China $7857 million

Top 5 importers of major arms, 1987–1991

India $17,561 million

Saudi Arabia $10,597 million

Iraq $10,319 million

Japan $9750 million

Afghanistan $8430 million

Children of war

The aftermath of war is visible: soldiers and civilians dead and injured; homes, water and sanitation systems destroyed; food supply lines broken. The psychological wounds are less visible. In a UNICEF survey of 50 displaced children in Mozambique, 42 had lost a mother or a father by violence, 11 had seen or heard a parent being killed, 29 had witnessed a murder, 16 had been kidnapped, all had been threatened, or beaten, or starved. The sample was considered to be "representative".

• Six hours' of military spending could pay to eradicate malaria, affecting 200 million people (UN).

• US studies show that spending $1 billion on guided missile production creates 9000 jobs: the same money spent on education would create 63,000 jobs (UN).

Tens of thousands of young people throughout the world fight alongside adult soldiers, such as this Somalian boy (right). Some join voluntarily, but others join to satisfy their needs for food and shelter. Many are forcibly recruited.

The remnants of war affect family life long after fighting has ceased. A high proportion of the 30 million mines sown in Afghanistan soil during the 1980s remain, ready to maim and kill children at play and adults at work. The costs of war have to be borne by governments as well as families for years after the fighting ceases. US research suggests that the medical and pension costs of wounded soldiers and other veterans tend to be almost three times the original outlay for a war.

The impact of war on families and communities is unmistakable. What is more difficult to see are the effects during peacetime preparations for war. Training armies, producing weapons, and exporting arms are all much less obvious in their impact. Yet, for example, the cost of training one soldier would educate 100 children in school. One new tank would finance 1000 classrooms for 30,000 developing world children. One Trident nuclear submarine would fund a global five-year child immunization programme to prevent one million deaths a year.

Overall, the governments of developing countries allocate around a quarter of their expenditure to the military. Soldiers outnumber doctors eight to one. Yet the chance of dying from social neglect, malnutrition, or preventable disease is 33 times greater than dying from war.

With the end of the Cold War the volume of arms on the international market has decreased, but the trade remains active – it is still the world's second largest industry, after oil. Three-quarters of the global arms trade involves exports to developing countries. The biggest military spenders are in the Middle East – Iraq, Israel, Oman, and Saudi Arabia being among those typically spending more than 10 per cent of GDP on the military.

Devoting large resources to the military has adverse consequences for domestic economies. The defence sector distorts the economy, channelling labour and other resources into unproductive activities. Aware of this some nations have made efforts to re-deploy military assets. Some 20 per cent of the output from China's 30,000 military factories, for example, has been converted to peaceful production.

Fortunately, sanity can break out amid armed hostilities. During the civil war in El Salvador fighting was suspended on three days each year for children to be immunized. In Sudan, Ethiopia, and Angola, "corridors of peace" were created through which essential supplies could reach millions of civilians, mostly women and children, trapped in the war zones. Stalemate, exhaustion, and war weariness have driven many combatants

soldiers outnumber doctors

Official figures for refugees suggest
there are at least 17 million globally –
people displaced from their own
country as a result of war, famine, and
political persecution. The map (right)
shows where the officially-recognized
refugees are. There may be as many as
30 million more who are displaced
within their own country.

"80 per cent of refugees are women and children"

to embrace the UN as a peacemaker. Since 1988 the UN has undertaken 13 peacekeeping missions – as many as in the whole of its previous 40-year history. Of these 13 missions, ten were charged with helping to resolve domestic conflicts and the transition to more democratic political systems.

Throughout the world millions of families are torn apart as war, political oppression, environmental collapse, and economic crises force them to migrate. People who manage to escape an afflicted zone and cross into a sympathetic neighbouring country may be able to join the 17 million with official refugee status. This entitles them to protection, food, and other forms of support from the international community. However, few come into this category – most enforced migrants are people who are displaced within their own country – a further 30 million.

Enforced migration from armed conflict has the most pernicious effect on family life. Some family members may stay behind, and others may be abducted or killed, while others may die before resettlement. It is estimated that around 80 per cent of refugees are women and children. Between three and five per cent are orphans or children separated from their families. Long-term displacement in refugee camps means children grow up with a distorted view of the outside world and they cannot learn practical skills such as farming or herding. In Cambodian refugee camps in Thailand, for example, traditional values have been replaced by modern "pop" camp culture.

dispossessed families

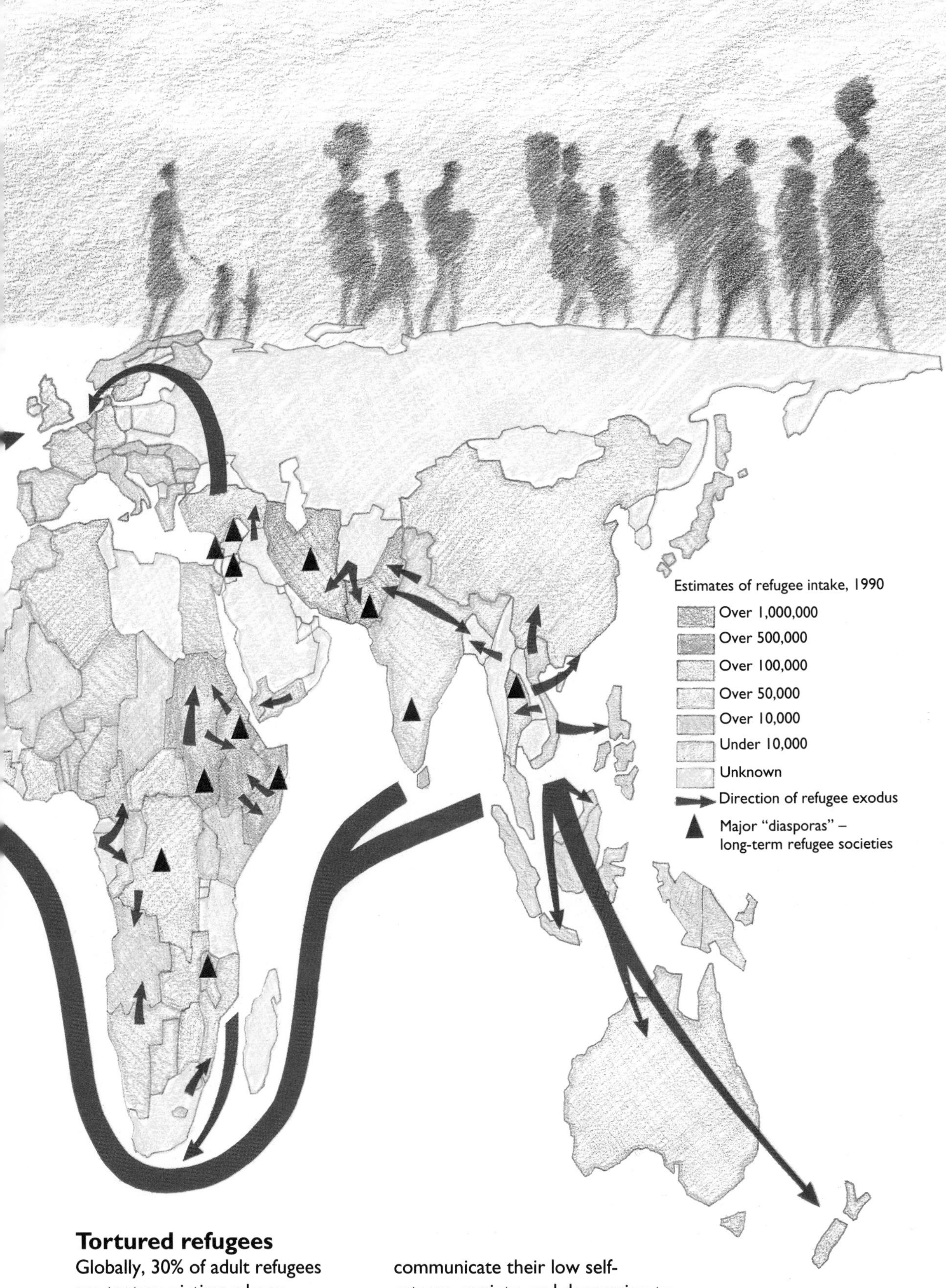

Estimates of refugee intake, 1990

Over 1,000,000
Over 500,000
Over 100,000
Over 50,000
Over 10,000
Under 10,000
Unknown
Direction of refugee exodus
Major "diasporas" –
long-term refugee societies

Tortured refugees

Globally, 30% of adult refugees are torture victims whose personalities are deeply damaged, according to the Rehabilitation and Research Centre for Torture Victims in Denmark. They may communicate their low self-esteem, anxiety, and depression to their children; they in turn can suffer from chronic fear, depressive moods, and poor school performance.

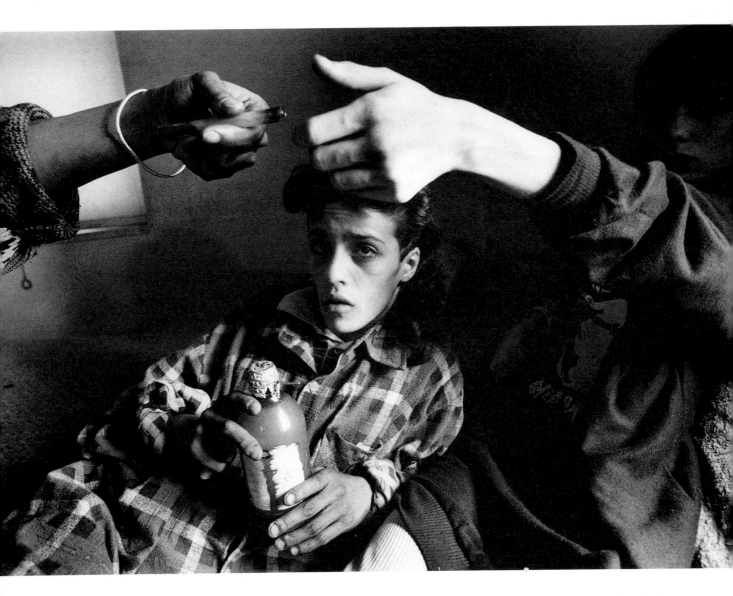

The epidemic of drug and alcohol abuse has spread all over the world. Some neighbourhoods are fully controlled by drugs gangs and users. "Crack" Annie (above) lives in such an area of Brooklyn, New York, in a crack den run by two girls. She supports her habit by prostitution. The whole neighbourhood has been drawn into drugs: entire families are addicted; the ice cream van sells crack.

Nearly all of the world's enforced migrants are in the developing world – half of them are in Africa. The poorest countries, such as Malawi, are host to some of the largest displaced populations. Meanwhile, rich industrialized countries in the North are closing their frontiers to asylum-seekers.

Drug and alcohol use are ancient habits in many parts of the world, frequently being used in religious ceremonies or for important social events. The coca leaf served as a stimulant in the Andean countries long before the Spanish conquest.

During this century, alcohol and illicit drug production, trafficking, and abuse have grown to epidemic proportions worldwide. The age at which abuse begins is declining rapidly, often caused by family stress and destitution. In some countries drug use begins as young as five years of age and many teenagers are fully addicted. Alcohol is also attractive to young people because it is often associated with toughness, rebelliousness, and acceptance by the peer group.

The social costs of alcohol and drug abuse are high, ranging from dangerous driving to theft and violence. Many addicts turn to crime to pay for supplies, and drug use is strongly linked with suicide attempts. The costs to family life are also heavy. In many Asian cities men prostitute their wives and daughters to pay for heroin.

Everywhere, availability and opportunity are the key ingredients for addiction. About 90 per cent of American soldiers addicted to heroin in Vietnam lost their addictions on returning to the US, because the drug was not so readily available. However, where illicit drugs are rare the use of solvents found in everyday materials take their place. In many cities young children can be found on the streets sniffing glue. The Brazilian authorities estimate that 80 per cent of the city's street children use drugs, shoemaker's glue being the most common.

While drugs consumption can destroy families, its production has played an important part in cushioning the economic crises facing hundreds of farming families and hired labourers. Colombia, Bolivia, and Peru produce 98 per cent of

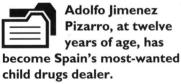

Adolfo Jimenez Pizarro, at twelve years of age, has become Spain's most-wanted child drugs dealer.

Adolfo comes from a gypsy family living on the outskirts of Madrid. Here, basic shelters of corrugated iron and planks of wood rival the dwellings of shanty towns in developing countries. His father, a heroin addict, has spent 18 years of his life in jail for drugs trafficking and is now in hospital with AIDS. His mother is in prison for drugs dealing and six siblings are in reform centres or behind bars.

There has been a relentless growth in Adolfo's association with drugs. His mother gave him mild drugs as an infant; he started on hard drugs at the age of six and was addicted within two years; at the age of ten he began peddling cocaine and heroin. He took over the family business with his older sister when his mother was jailed. For his quickness, toughness, and capacity to survive in an unsavoury environment, he has been nicknamed "Little Rat".

Adolfo has been caught several times by the police. He has been sent to remand homes – and escaped each time. Adolfo's father argues that there is no alternative to drugs dealing for gypsies, as they are not allowed to carry out their traditional trade of selling wares in markets, or door to door. "We have no decent houses and no means of earning a living. What can you expect? We have to use our children to help us".

The chain of cause and effect has many links: discrimination against gypsies and social neglect lead to family hardship, few survival options, and exploitation by parents. A further, disturbing element is exploitation by the media. Little Rat's exploits have brought the press to the gypsy encampment, helping to turn Adolfo into a local and national hero – admired and emulated by other children.

coca leaves for the international cocaine market. Although most of the profits are taken out of the region by drugs traders, it is estimated that the combined income from cocaine to these countries is more than $1 billion annually.

The use of intravenous drugs, particularly heroin, is a major cause in the transmission of the human immunodeficiency virus (HIV). The effects of drugs on the family are amplified by the risk of HIV and AIDS infection.

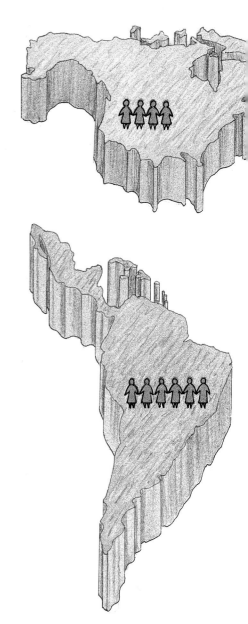

HIV was unknown to science until its discovery in 1981, and by the end of 1992 had infected almost 13 million people according to the US-based Global Aids Policy Coalition. Most people remain healthy for many years but eventually become vulnerable to a range of infections, and finally develop AIDS. Some 2.6 million of those infected by HIV have so far developed AIDS; 2.5 million of these have died. As yet medical science has no means to stop this devastating personal and social process.

Throughout the world HIV and AIDS has ravaged family life. For example, when an income earner becomes ill a heavy economic burden is placed on the family. Often, financial resources are completely eroded, and medical treatment is frequently unaffordable. Since an infected person may unknowingly pass on the virus to sexual partners, both parents of a family may become sick.

Women account for more than four million of the worldwide total of HIV infections, and their proportion is growing. Three-quarters of all infections are caused by heterosexual intercourse, but in many cultures women have no power to abstain from sex or persuade their partners to use condoms for protection. This can kill them and the children they bear.

Almost one-third of HIV infected mothers give birth to children unable to develop immunity against routine infections. More than one million HIV infected children have already been born and 80 per cent will die before reaching the age of five. They desperately need special care during their short lives.

As the number of young fathers and mothers dying from AIDS-related illnesses increases, so does the number of orphans. By 2000, the World Health Organization estimates that about 10 million children worldwide will have lost parents to AIDS. Today, in regions of Uganda, families of as many as 14 children are being cared for by aged grandparents because the parents have fallen victim to AIDS.

HIV and children

In many societies, the bearing of sons gives a woman status and pregnancy is often not avoided. This remains true when the woman is HIV-positive. In areas where 1 in 4 children die before they are 5 years old, the added risk of passing on HIV is no deterrent. In Kigali, Rwanda, UNICEF estimates that the number of HIV-positive pregnant women rose from 18% in 1986 to 30% in 1989.

HIV, AIDS, and families

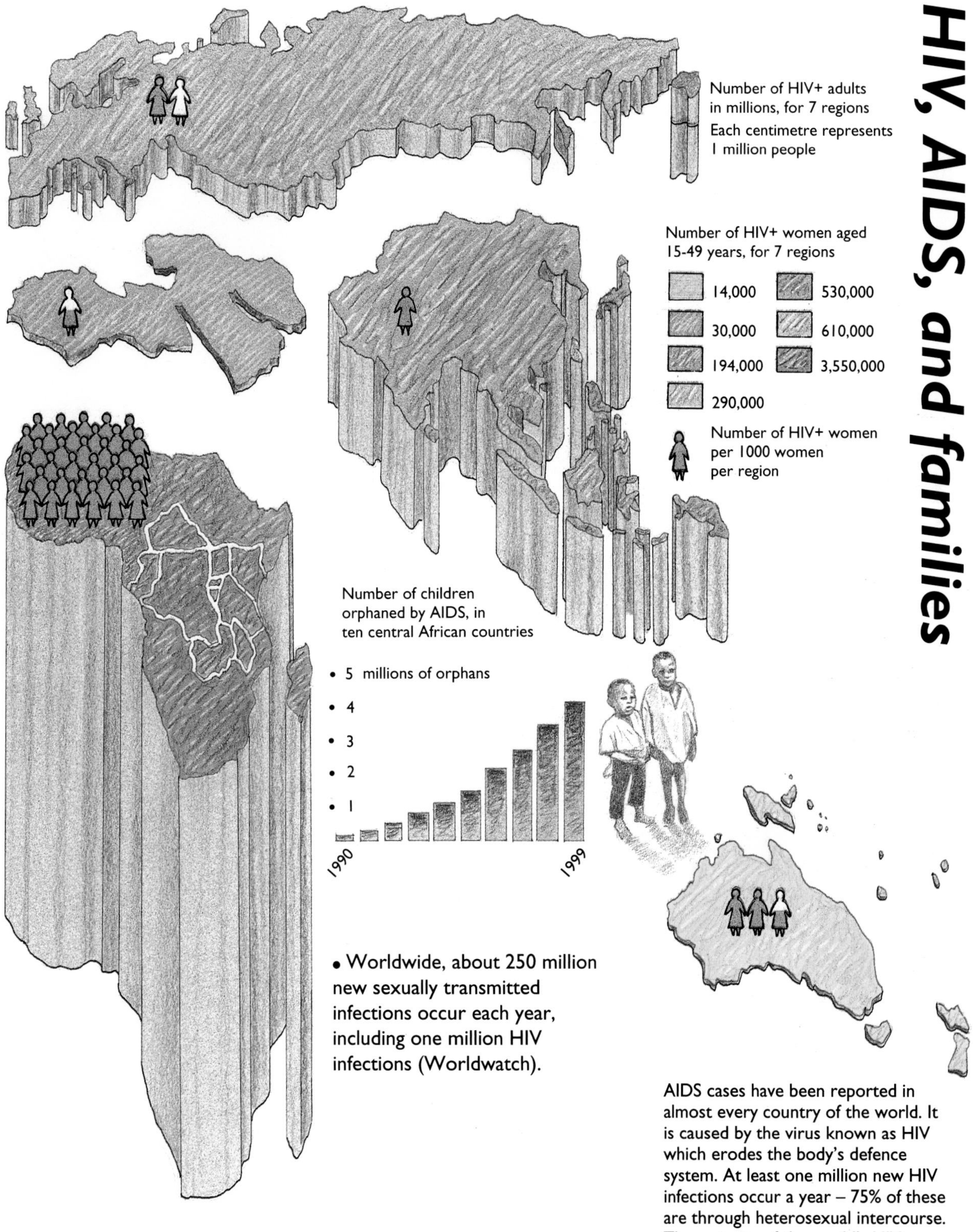

Number of HIV+ adults
in millions, for 7 regions

Each centimetre represents
1 million people

Number of HIV+ women aged
15-49 years, for 7 regions

14,000	530,000
30,000	610,000
194,000	3,550,000
290,000	

Number of HIV+ women
per 1000 women
per region

Number of children
orphaned by AIDS, in
ten central African countries

- 5 millions of orphans
- 4
- 3
- 2
- 1

1990   1999

- Worldwide, about 250 million
new sexually transmitted
infections occur each year,
including one million HIV
infections (Worldwatch).

AIDS cases have been reported in
almost every country of the world. It
is caused by the virus known as HIV
which erodes the body's defence
system. At least one million new HIV
infections occur a year – 75% of these
are through heterosexual intercourse.
The majority of the world's HIV
sufferers are in the developing regions
(above). AIDS cuts down men and
women in their prime, leaving orphans
and the aged, and profound social and
economic consequences.

*"Almost one-third of HIV infected
mothers give birth to HIV+ children"*

In many regions information and education on protection against AIDS is scarce. In Uganda, however, the schools programme has been revised to include AIDS prevention. It has been so successful that the teaching resources have been translated and adapted for other African countries. Popular campaigns through television, radio, and posters have been developed throughout the world. HIV and AIDS represent one of the greatest challenges yet to society's capacity for love and compassion.

Planning the human family

We are living at a time of the fastest ever growth in human numbers. UN projections suggest that by 2050 the world's population will have reached 10 billion, almost twice that of today, and that it will reach 11.6 billion a century later. This "most probable" prediction assumes that fertility will fall to the level at which couples replace themselves with children, and no further. But in most developed and in a handful of developing countries, fertility has fallen below this level. No one knows whether such levels will remain low in these nations, or if all countries will experience a similar decline in fertility. There can be no guarantees in a world riddled with pockets of poverty and conflict.

While Europe's population took 300 years to double, in many parts of Africa and Asia it takes only 50 years. These dramatic trends in population growth became apparent in the 1960s. They were partly caused by a decline in death rates following successful campaigns against killer diseases such as malaria and tuberculosis, and improvements in public health. Parents' fears that many of their children would die had yet to be dispelled. Some referred to it as a "population crisis". Meanwhile, countries had the onerous and expensive task of creating new schools, hospitals, and jobs to keep up with increasing numbers of people.

Because most population growth is occurring in the developing world, while concern over human numbers overwhelming the Earth's fragile resources comes from the industrialized nations, debates about the population crisis are deeply contentious. But balancing population against resources is misleading because it assumes each person in the world consumes the same. Yet one-quarter of the world's population living in the industrialized nations consume 75 per cent of the world's energy. The average person in such a country is responsible for 20 times more water and air pollutants than the counterpart in the developing world. Assuming current trends do not change, the

A birth is a cause for celebration. Too many births may be a cause for alarm. The decade of the 1990s is seeing the highest annual additions to world population in all history. The UN estimates that by the year 2000 no less than 969 million people will have been added over the decade. This is equivalent to adding the population of New York every two months (above).

the population issue

57.5 million extra people born in the industrialized countries in the 1990s will actually create more pollution than the extra 911 million in the developing world. And matters will gradually worsen as the latter begin to demand and get a modern, industrial life style.

Contraception is one strategy, albeit controversial, to limit population growth. Some religions outlaw any unnatural means of contraception and in many societies – both modern and developing – the young are denied any effective sex education. Clearly, this is one way ahead and an area which can be

One child in China
Chinese government policy requires couples to bear only one child. Social researchers have identified a number of problems facing one-child families: the tendency of parents and relatives to spoil an only son or daughter; the only child is inclined to be wilful and unsociable; the child also has fewer peers and no siblings to assist the socialization process.

significantly improved. It should certainly prove more effective than impersonal state controls. The Indian government's population policy of he 1970s inspired such immense popular resistance that its impact was damaged. Even China has found its one-child policy difficult to implement.

A crucial element in slowing population growth is the availability of "family planning" – the option to choose family size by effective and convenient methods. The term "family planning" is often used interchangeably with "contraception" and is taken to mean the deliberate avoidance of pregnancy. Throughout history,child-bearing has often been a cultural, not just a private matter. The ideal of virginity before marriage, and chastity within it, is one example. In the past a sound family planning strategy tended to maximize healthy reproduction instead of curtailing it. Since many children would die, more pregnancies, not fewer, were needed.

The health risks to women from regular, frequent child birth are particularly high in poor countries. The Nilots in Sudan are among the communities to recognize this and believe it wrong to have another child before the first is weaned. In some Pacific islands the decision whether a woman should have an abortion or continue with a pregnancy is made by the village chief, the community's ability to support another child taking precedence over the mother's health.

The use of modern contraceptives has increased very dramatically in developing countries. In 1960 only nine per cent of women were using them, but the figure increased to 50 per cent by 1990. There has also been a correspondingly steep decline in fertility, from 6.1 to 3.9 births per woman. The decline, however, has been uneven in different regions of the world, the steepest being in east Asia, and the smallest in Africa.

Reducing population growth is not, however, just a matter of increasing access to contraception. It involves a very broad spectrum of measures hinging around child health, and women's freedom to decide their destinies and control their fertilities.

The WHO estimates that there are still some 300 million couples in the world who do not desire any more children, but who do not have access to family planning services. The unmet need for family planning is borne out by the desperate measures taken by some women such as the immense numbers of illegal and often dangerous abortions performed each year.

Birth prevention worldwide

Sterilization, IUDs, and the "pill" account for 70% of contraceptive use worldwide. WHO estimates that sterilization is the most commonly practised form of birth control, representing one-third of world contraceptive use. More than half of all those sterilized live in China and India. Research by WHO also reveals that Japan has the highest rate of condom use: in 1986, 69% of all couples practising contraception used condoms.

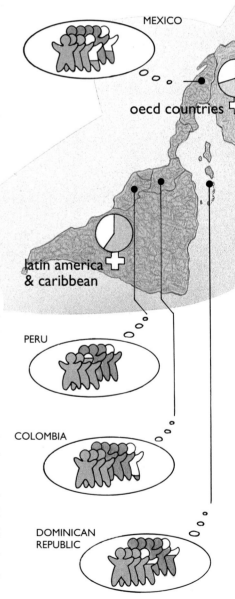

About one-third of married women in the developing world are using modern family planning methods (below). Social factors, such as women's access to education, are also reducing family size. Women's desires, especially, are reflected by surveys carried out in the 1970s and 1980s showing a reduction in the number of children women want.

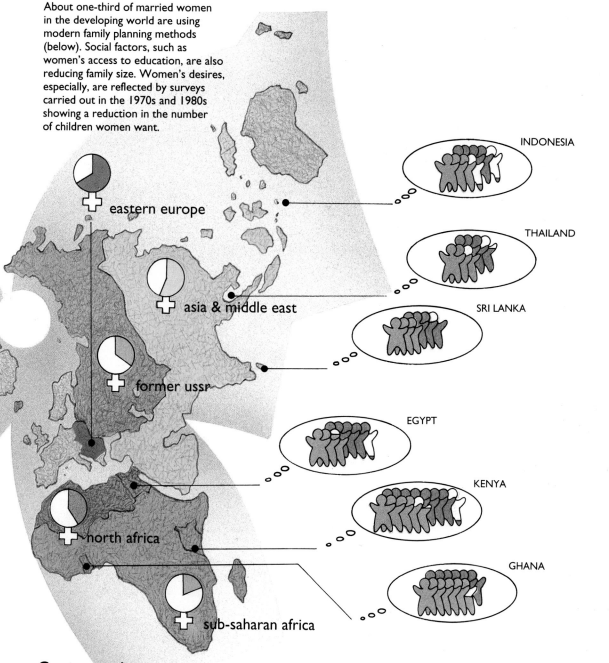

eastern europe

asia & middle east

former ussr

north africa

sub-saharan africa

INDONESIA

THAILAND

SRI LANKA

EGYPT

KENYA

GHANA

Contraceptive controversy

Norplant, a surgically implanted contraceptive device, was approved by the US Food and Drug Administration in 1990. Considered the biggest development in birth control since the "pill" in the 1960s, it became the most controversial when a Baltimore high school offered the drug to its students in 1993.

Average number of children desired by married women

Orange figures represent numbers desired in the 1970s; green figures represent those desired in the 1980s

OECD is the Organization for Economic Co-operation and Development

Percentage of married women of child-bearing age using contraception, for 7 regions, 1990

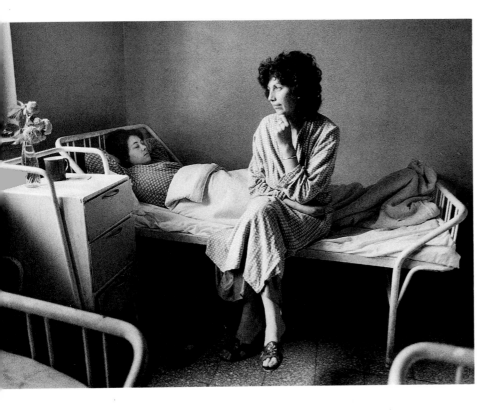

Romania has Europe's highest ratio of abortions to live births. Three babies are terminated for every one born. In this Bucharest maternity hospital (left) one woman waits for an abortion while the other recovers from one. Both share the same bed.

 Pro-life arguments against abortion continue to confront the conviction that women must have the right to choose. The debate is endlessly complicated by health, moral, ethical, and religious attitudes. Laws vary widely from one country to another.

In Ireland in 1992, for example, the parents of a 14-year-old girl won the legal right for her to travel to England and have an unwanted pregnancy – the result of rape – terminated.

Conversely, in Italy in 1993, Carla Levati Ardenghi refused cancer treatment for fear that it would damage her unborn baby. She died in childbirth and her baby son died ten days later, leaving her husband to raise their ten-year-old child on his own. He had backed his wife's decision not to have an abortion or chemotherapy.

This brave choice was praised by the Italian press; "She defeated death and affirmed the idea of maternity as immortality." However, women's rights campaigners are worried that pro-life groups will use the case to encourage the repeal of the 1978 law that allows Italian women to have an abortion during the first three months of pregnancy.

Even now, with abortion widely practised in Italy, it can be difficult to arrange legally. Doctors who declare themselves "conscientious objectors" can refuse any involvement in performing abortions. The pro-life campaigners are motivated by the desire to protect the right to life of the unborn – and many fear an increase in abortions in industrialized countries.

abortion

Abortion has long been used as a form of "birth control" in traditional societies throughout the world. This is often ignored by policy-makers who think that family size in traditional cultures goes unchecked. In places where reliable contraception is not available and infanticide is taboo, abortion often becomes a means of controlling family growth. Knowledge of the abortive properties of plants is extensive in many cultures. In Trinidad, for instance, pregnant women abstain from eating pineapples and unripe mangoes for this reason.

In countries with restrictive family planning policies women may have up to 20 abortions during their reproductive years. For every birth in Moscow a woman has between two and six legal abortions, and for every three legal abortions she has an illegal one. Illegal abortions – often carried out in unsterile conditions with rudimentary skills and equipment – can kill. Of the 500,000 women who die every year from causes related to pregnancy and childbirth, up to 200,000 result from poorly-performed, septic abortions.

During this century women have sought to control their fertility by gaining access to contraception and to legalized, safe abortion. But they continue to meet resistance from those who argue that human life begins at the moment of conception, and that the rights of women are subservient to the rights of the embryo and immature fetus. In most Western countries, however, and increasingly in the developing world, the right of women to terminate pregnancy during early gestation has won legislative endorsement.

"Up to 200,000 women die each year from ill-performed abortions"

Reductions in the abortion rate, which would both reduce the maternal death rate and the number of women whose child-bearing prospects are damaged by unsafe procedures, can only be achieved by improving access to contraception. Yet strongly Catholic countries, such as Ireland, the Philippines, and Brazil, are still reluctant. In Brazil government policy limits access to reversible contraceptives such as condoms and diaphragms; as a result 41 per cent of contraceptive users are sterilized. Women who find this unacceptable see no alternative but abortion – a criminal offence. There are estimated to be 4 million abortions a year in Brazil, perhaps a tenth of the world total.

• In 1992, seven US women aged between 50 and 59 became pregnant after successful operations grafted the fertilized eggs of younger donors.

• In 1987, 3000 frozen embryos were stored in the UK, with 10,000 in storage worldwide.

Where family planning services are available many programmes exclude teenagers and unmarried women, despite evidence that these groups are most likely to have unwanted pregnancies. Few family planning clinics offer abortions or are equipped to treat the damage caused by ill-performed abortions.

The women's movement has very real fears about scientific intervention in the reproductive process. Women's only vestige of power in a male dominated society is their monopoly of child-bearing. The creation of life artificially and the scientific prospect – however remote – of male pregnancy breaks this monopoly. Yet, others believe that new technologies will liberate women, making it possible for them to become mothers – biologically and socially – without going through pregnancy and birth.

Some experts predict that male pregnancy may become a reality in the future. Society is probably not ready for such a dramatic development, yet there could be a time when a couple decide that the man should become pregnant rather than his partner because it suits him to take a career break or because she is earning more. This kind of choice might herald an equality in parenting relationships never before imagined.

Bizarre possibilities such as male pregnancy can detract attention from the major medical advantages arising from innovation in reproductive technologies. The prospects of cures for genetic abnormalities, birth defects, infertility, miscarriages, still births, and neonatal deaths all spur scientists on in their research. Some medical scientists fear that a public backlash against embryo research could result in legal restrictions curbing discovery in the area of genetic disease.

"Couples pay up to $2000 at gender clinics to choose their child's sex before conception"

For many people new procedures such as artificial insemination and *in-vitro* fertilization give the scientists a moral dilemma. Reproductive technologies raise a multitude of legal and ethical complications and may have unintended social consequences. Treatments such as *in-vitro* fertilization and fertility drugs increase maternal and fetal health risks during the

pregnancy because of their association with multiple births. Miscarriage is particularly common and social isolation, poverty, and family stress can result from multiple births. Amniocentesis, now widely used to determine the sex of the fetus, is leading to the widespread abortion of female fetuses. At clinics across Europe, Asia, and America couples can even pay up to $2000 at "gender clinics" to choose their child's sex before conception.

Commercial surrogacy is another controversial practice made possible by technological advance. Surrogate mothers are harangued for making procreation a business and are accused of having no maternal instinct when they give up the baby. But when a surrogate mother decides she will not relinquish her infant who has the greater right to the child – the surrogate or the "commissioning" mother? Though we should be grateful for medical advances, we have also got to learn how and when to use them. Technology requires enormous responsibility.

Life in his hands. A flask containing the medium for nurturing human eggs is held by Dr Roger Gosden (above). His work on freezing ovaries will make it possible to store vast numbers of human eggs. Egg banks could help overcome the shortage of eggs for donation to women who have had a premature menopause. Dr Gosden's team is also preparing to transplant ovaries. Ovary grafts could treat infertility, protect fertility, and delay the menopause.

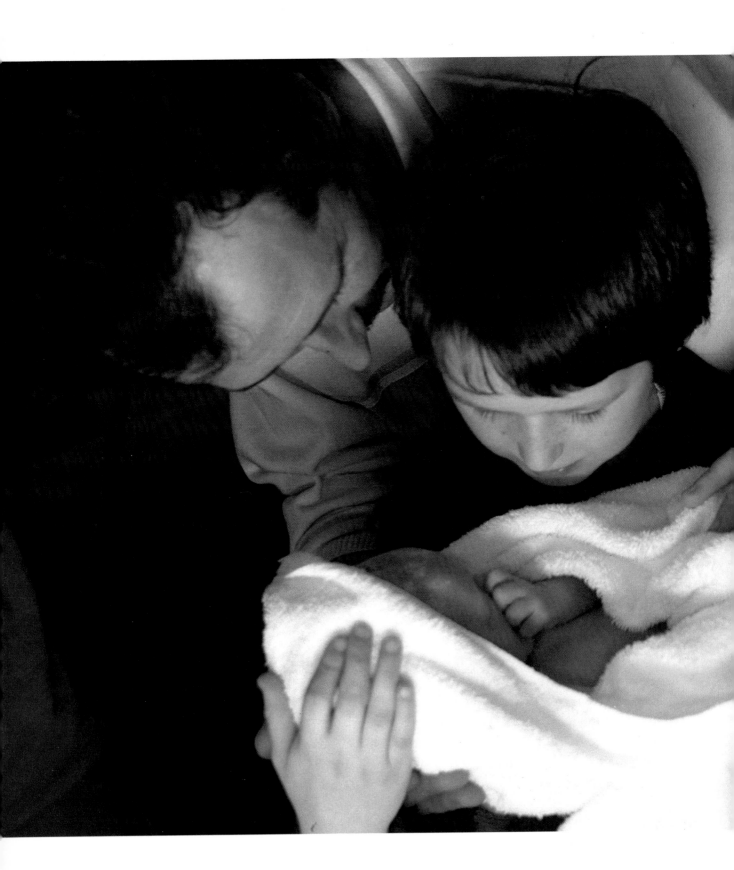

meeting the challenge

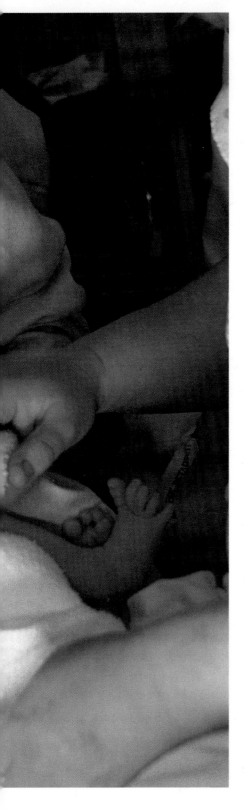

The reasons for family problems do not lie solely in families. Neither are the solutions to these problems solely in their hands. This final part focuses on how we can create a more "friendly" society for all families.

It shows that the aim is to create an environment in which families may act on their own behalf. They are experts in their own affairs and should be partners in decision-making. The most effective public policies prevent crises as far as possible, and rehabilitate those in need of special help. They build on the family's strengths rather than react to weaknesses.

The challenge of creating a family-friendly society is one of achieving a balance. How far can the rights of individuals be promoted while respecting the privacy of the family? What will be the most effective balance between state intervention, voluntary support, and private aid? How will policy makers balance fostering "traditional" family forms with alternative ways of living?

A family-friendly society is one that understands and safeguards the rights of *all* families. The sheer diversity of family forms is a universal and historical feature of society – an enriching force in human understanding and development.

Birth: a new life brings with it new hopes, and changes for all family members (left).

The family plays a central role in the safeguarding of cultural heritage (above) despite rapidly changing social patterns.

In partnership with families

Families – with their rich diversity of forms and functions – remain the central institution in society. Now, in the final decade of this century, policy-makers throughout the world are trying to create a safer and healthier environment for them; a supportive environment that will enable families to function to the very best of their abilities.

Acknowledging this need, and the growing acceptance that human development is a more appropriate goal than economic advance alone, the United Nations General Assembly proclaimed 1994 as the International Year of the Family. One particularly important objective is protecting and furthering the rights of individual family members. Following the Convention on the Elimination of All Forms of Discrimination against Women and the Nairobi Forward-looking Strategies for the Advancement of Women, fostering equality between women and men is high on the agenda. So too is the aim to ensure that children, people with disabilities, and the elderly will be well provided for in the family.

In much of the world, the harshest threats to family life stem, at root, from inequalities in the global economic order. These inequalities are a major cause of the environmental damage, political instability, enforced migration, and armed conflict that affect so many families in developing countries today. The world community needs clear, bold strategies, which address the fundamental causes of such problems, not merely the symptoms. We need to target environmental sustainability; food security; resource redistribution; economic adjustment that safeguards the poor; further reductions in population growth; and solutions to conflict. The problems are great. Paradoxically, the key to solving them lies in their most frequent victim, the family itself. Policies that support the family are the first step. To develop such essential strategies governments need the support of international organizations such as the World Bank and the UN agencies, of non-governmental organizations, and of the community groups working with families every day.

safeguarding the future

"To raise funds for family welfare, arms expenditure can be redirected and debt repayments rescheduled"

Governments passing new legislation now need to give priority to the key family issues. These include support for the poorest and most vulnerable; equal conditions of employment for men and women and paid parental leave; divorce settlements, alimony and child support measures; and inheritance and property rights. And to raise extra funds for the social sector generally, and family welfare in particular, arms expenditure can be redirected and debt repayments re-scheduled. We also need more research, because many family issues are poorly understood. A further vital step would be to replace cumbersome,

• US and Russian nuclear warheads are estimated to fall from 57,000 in 1988 to 12,000 by the year 2000 (Worldwatch).

• Between 1948 and 1992 the UN spent $8.3 billion on peacekeeping, compared to about $30 trillion spent by the world's governments on the military.

centralized bureaucracy with far more responsive and flexible local services. These steps, taken together, will release the human potential to create a brighter future.

In the past, in industrialized societies, the demands on the family were different. Early entry into the labour force, high infant mortality, and shorter life expectancy resulted in relatively low numbers of dependants. Now all that has changed; families often have to care for dependent children for 20 years or more, rearing literate, responsible individuals who can succeed in a world increasingly shaped by high technology; as well as care for disabled and elderly family members.

Such pressure means many families need extra help. But who should provide and fund it? In socialist countries the answer is the public sector. In liberal democracies aid comes from central and local government *and* from private enterprise, including religious and community groups, private foundations, welfare agencies, and employers.

Striking the right balance between public sector intervention, voluntary effort, and private aid is vital if needy families are not to slip through the safety net. And it is a balance

 In Zimbabwe, the Zimcare Trust has introduced a "home-operated programme of education for children with individual learning difficulties". This government-supported initiative has demonstrated the skill of parents as educators and the importance of participation by the family.

There are at least 10,000 mentally handicapped children in Zimbabwe; mostly from poor families living in rural areas, far from specialist services. Existing institutions only met a fraction of the need, and isolated children from their families and communities. The Zimcare Trust and the ministries of health and education agreed that their aim should be to help children take part as fully as possible in family and community life.

The scheme works through home teachers drawn from a variety of backgrounds – teachers, health workers, family, and friends – who attend a three-day training session. The home teacher begins by talking to the family and local community leaders, listening to their concerns and learning about their attitudes toward mental handicap. In further meetings the programme is explained and children are assessed.

The home teacher is expected to negotiate the time and length of visits with the family and adapt to its life style. Realistic, relevant goals are selected with the family; priority is given to practical survival skills. A mentally handicapped child who learns how to perform everyday, domestic tasks will earn respect in the community and feel a greater sense of confidence and self-worth. Between visits by the home teacher, the parents have information cards to refer to as they continue the teaching task.

The programme has clearly shown that a partnership with parents is productive and warmly welcomed when the content and context are suited to the needs of the child, the family, and the wider community.

which is constantly changing. The current world recession and the growth of free market principles in the social sector means public funding is now declining in many countries. Consequently welfare has become big business. In Canada the private sector now manages some 40 per cent of beds in residential homes and 60 per cent in nursing homes. And in the US half of all beds are controlled by a handful of private companies. But there are potential drawbacks.

What happens to poor families who cannot afford essential services such as health insurance in the USA? Why should families in industrialized countries pay for services that were once free? Furthermore, conditions in private institutions are sometimes poor; the desire for profits may take precedence over quality. Standards of care set by the state are sometimes difficult to enforce. What happens when neither the state nor the private sector can provide?

There are new solutions emerging. Gaps in some public services have led to the growth of innovative pilot schemes, often managed by non-government bodies. In the US, where public welfare is restricted and belief in individual freedom and private enterprise is strong, voluntary self-help groups now do an excellent job helping the needy. The most extensive growth of such services is in developing countries. In Papua New Guinea, for example, disabled people are now cared for not just by the handful of resident physiotherapists but by a large network of local para-professionals.

• In São Paulo, Brazil, there are at least 1300 neighbourhood associations working to improve the life of urban families.

"Publicising the need for family health care is a key issue"

Publicising the need for family health care is another innovation. Often publicity is at its most effective when voiced by celebrities such as the late Audrey Hepburn, a UNICEF "goodwill ambassador" who promoted primary health measures in many developing countries. Such popular media figures are particularly good at getting the message over to the young. The media has also successfully communicated positive messages of, and for, the family, especially in the fight against AIDS, highlighting the importance of safe sex. In fact, the greater the range of family problems, the greater the need to find innovative ways of responding from the public and private sector. Between them they can become an enormous force for good.

• In Lima's shanty towns, women's self-help groups run at least 1500 community kitchens.

• In Sri Lanka, the village awakening movement mobilizes three million people in activities from education to road building.

sharing responsibility

Social planners are often wary of giving benefits to families that do not fit conventional patterns, in case this should reinforce a swing away from traditional families. State benefits and rights may be made conditional on legal unions, for example, to encourage people to marry. But this approach puts at a disadvantage children and adults living in informal family arrangements. Adoption, too, may be restricted to young heterosexual couples with stable incomes, on the grounds that this is the best context for bringing up children. This policy has reduced the supply of potential adoptive families, especially for older children or for those who have disabilities. These children may need to live with people who have a special commitment to parenting regardless of their domestic arrangements.

The questions for social planners are: should they help promote conventional family structures? Should they support families who chose to live differently? And can they fund these lifestyles? An even broader question is: how far should the state provide social care in support of families, if at all?

Some policy-makers clearly want families to meet more of their needs themselves. But with the current trend away from the extended family, and both parents working, there is increasing public demand for support facilities such as state child care.

Western policy makers are increasingly facing the question of how far to support "non-traditional" families (above, left). In many other regions, however, there are few state provisions and communities themselves are at the forefront in providing support for their families. This soup kitchen (above, right) is run co-operatively by the families of a Peruvian shanty town.

strength in change

"How far should the state provide social care in support of families?"

In Canada, the US, and the UK, government is making its position quite clear. Large state institutions for disabled people and the elderly are being closed, in favour of residential and support services within the community and families. At worst, the family and community may be seen by government as a cheap alternative to public welfare. But that need not be the

Education on family matters and available services is an essential way of promoting the welfare of individual members. Teaching parents about hygiene and good nutrition, for example, can dramatically improve the wellbeing of their children (above).

case. Provided full and sensitive support is given, such policy changes can enhance the inherent strengths of families and help them meet the demands of modern society.

Numerous other advances are now evident in family trends. In many countries, girls are expecting and getting the same opportunities as boys; there is growing public attention to domestic violence; and in countries such as Sweden unmarried couples with children benefit from strong legal obligations to each other.

Empowering families

In national policy development, governments often focus on meeting economic, political, military, or demographic goals. Rarely is family welfare a priority. Yet policy needs to be assessed for its impact on family life, particularly on the vulnerable. Every civilized society recognizes that a comprehensive range of interventions is required to safeguard family rights and welfare. Statutory provision may take many forms, from free or subsidized services to cash allowances or tax relief. In most countries with a comprehensive policy, a healthy balance is struck between financial support and service provision.

The aim is to meet universal requirements such as health care, housing, and education, while also providing for families with special needs. The priority in education is generally to make available free schooling as well as special services for those with learning disabilities. Health care is provided by a growing number of preventive primary health care measures, such as community clinics and doctors, and supported by secondary services such as hospitals. Equally, it is important to guard against reduction or loss of earnings through unemployment or sickness. Major life changes such as pregnancy and birth, childrearing, retirement, and bereavement tend to bring a fall in family income and incur extra expenditure. States can provide financial assistance from social insurance contributions, by giving unconditional support to specific target groups, and by assessing the family's needs in relation to its financial resources.

The industrialized countries all have statutory social policies, with varying degrees of state involvement. However, developing countries often fall short of their social sector goals through lack of funds. There are few public welfare institutions, and social security is only now being introduced. In these areas most welfare work is conducted by non-government bodies. Even in those countries, such as Brazil, where public expenditure on the social sector is relatively high, the poor distribution of services leads to neglect of rural families and those living in urban slums.

To be effective, service provision and financial benefits need a strong commitment to complementary measures – educating the general public on family matters, available services, and benefits. Fostering both knowledge and caring values within the family is the surest way to protect and promote the rights and welfare of individual members. The health and wellbeing of young children, for example, is dramatically improved by teaching parents about birth spacing, hygiene, good nutrition, and safety within the home. Informed families can help prevent disability, alcohol and drug addiction, violence, and neglect. They can also cater for the special needs of disabled members by learning basic rehabilitation techniques.

More rights for parents and children

The UK Children Act 1989 aims to reduce state interference with family life except where necessary for the child's welfare. Under the emergency protection order, courts can authorize the removal of a child at risk for up to eight days. Parents can challenge the order in court after 72 hours. This replaces the 28-day place of safety order with no right of parental challenge.

Since women are primarily responsible for child-rearing and domestic matters, most family policy and information on family welfare is targeted at them. But programmes to involve men in family life are badly needed, if only to ensure the fair distribution of responsibilities. Once this might have seemed an impossible task. Fortunately that is no longer the case.

Low pre-school provision
In the UK only only one in twelve children under five years have access to a nursery place or registered childminder. Provision is slightly better for the older pre-school child, but still only a quarter of three- and four-year-olds are in nursery education compared to over 95% in France.

The welfare of the family in the modern state is closely linked to employment and income. Controlling unemployment, sustaining viable rates of pay, credit provision, job creation, and training are important safeguards against impoverishment.

As a growing number of women join the labour force, and return to work after having children, the relationship between work and family is thrown into sharp relief. For example, during the last 25 years the employment of women in the US has increased by a third in every age category up to 55 years, while men's employment has declined in every age group above 25 years. This trend represents a profound shift in life styles and work patterns, and contradicts many of society's long-held assumptions. There are strong economic forces behind such shifts. For a great majority of young two-parent families, it is no longer possible for one wage earner to provide for the household – dual worker families are an increasing trend in North America and Europe.

"Both women and men should be given greater choice about how they balance their work and family lives"

Some of the most obvious implications of such shifts involve the support given to working parents. As with service provision, the question with such support is: who should provide it? The state or the private sector? One goal might be to ensure that sufficient state child care and "elder care" is available. But by modifying the organization of employment itself, both women and men may be given greater choice about how they balance their work and family lives. Employers can play their part by introducing flexible working schedules – including part-time, job sharing, term-time, and twilight shifts – enabling parents and those with adult dependants to adjust work

● In Denmark, more than 48% of children under three years of age attend a nursery.

family-friendly work

demands to home responsibilities. Allowing people to work from home is another positive step. In the US tax allowances are available for "teleworkers" who use new technology to work from home. Some 27 million of the 126.4 million US workforce have telecommuted at some time. Providing for career breaks, such as maternity and paternity leave, without letting them jeopardize opportunities for promotion, is another crucial element. Emphasis can also be placed on assisting parents to re-enter the workforce by offering child care in the workplace. Adapting the opening hours of service facilities such as health centres and child care units also benefits family welfare.

The gains of introducing family friendly measures far outweigh the costs: employers are able to retain skilled workers, attract a wider pool of applicants, reduce labour turnover, and match labour supply more effectively to demand. For women, family-friendly measures are vital. They improve access to employment, generally, and help to remove women's handicap in the jobs market, when they are the ones who work part-time or leave employment for several years to raise the family. Supportive employers can also provide positive options for men,

In the absence of action by employers and state, working parents find solutions to their child care needs. This Mexican creche (above) is run by a union for domestic workers.

Wanted: children separated from their families by the war in Mozambique (above). These posters are part of a tracing programme that attempts to reunite shattered families.

• The UK telephone help line, Parentline, receives at least 50 calls a day.

• A programme to provide traditional birth attendants to 41 villages in the Indian state of Orissa in the 1980s halved the rate of maternal deaths.

to help them create closer bonds with their children, and to forge a climate of opinion in which men are seen as active parents sharing domestic responsibilities with women.

Measures to tackle serious family crises – abandonment, abuse and neglect, and marital breakdown – are essential in all societies. Timely and sensitive intervention during periods of stress can avert crisis. "Childline" in the UK, for example, helps children deal with problems such as bullying, sexual abuse, alcohol and drug addiction, and truancy. Much of its work entails listening and helping antagonists to see each others' perspective.

In cases of maltreatment and violence in the family the UN has called for policies that are preventive, and which offer immediate protection and assistance. Crisis intervention is handled by a broad mix of voluntary groups, religious bodies, and state agencies. The media often play a key role in bringing issues to public attention and thus triggering the formation of new policies and new care organizations. When tackling family crises, however, all agencies face the choice of whether to use the law to protect the sufferer, or to try more therapeutic approaches, such as conciliation, mediation, and peace-making.

Criminal law is punitive rather than rehabilitative and some social researchers and policy-makers believe that arrest, prosecution, and sentencing are unsuitable for domestic matters. In some countries it is reported that social workers try to persuade victims of domestic violence not to go to court. But violence against women is a repeated pattern and usually increases in severity over time, so this is hardly a solution.

"Conciliation services and family courts encourage collaboration between couples"

When the Minneapolis US Police Department compared the effectiveness of mediation with arrest and overnight imprisonment as methods of dealing with men who had abused their partners, the more punitive approach was found to reduce re-offending. By contrast, when dealing with family breakdown and divorce, it is now generally accepted that adversarial methods cause avoidable suffering to both adults and children. Recognizing this, conciliation services and family courts have been established in many countries to minimize hostile attitudes and encourage collaboration between couples.

 A child's "innocent" world can be shattered at a brutally young age. When Cathy was only three years old she began exhibiting excessive sexual behaviour, and her nanny took her to an NSPCC Child Protection Team. The NSPCC (National Society for the Prevention of Cruelty to Children) is one of the UK's leading child welfare organizations. An investigation found that the nanny's brother had been sexually abusing the child.

Play therapy, especially the use of puppets, gradually enabled Cathy to describe her ordeal and to release her fear, bewilderment, anger, and hurt. The abuser had made her believe that if she revealed the abuse she would be eaten alive by rats; hours of patient work were required to reassure her that the rats were imaginary.

The NSPCC therapist helped Cathy to understand that certain parts of her body were private; she had the right to shout "no" if anyone tried to touch them.

Secrecy is one of the hallmarks of child sexual abuse, especially where the abuser is a parent or close family member. Adults, unable to talk when they were abused as children, have described the fear of everything falling apart if they revealed the truth. Feelings of betrayal and hurt may become too painful to articulate; or the confusion of experiencing both love and abuse may lead the child to grow up in the belief that one goes with the other. Through the therapist, Cathy's family was helped to support her and encourage her not to keep secrets.

Domestic violence and child abuse will not be solved by legal means alone. Attitudes and relationships within society and the family have first to change. In many countries there are now awareness-raising campaigns that focus on these issues. There are also measures to increase equality between women and men in their roles as sexual partners, spouses, and parents, and to promote the rights of children within the family. The message "share responsibility, don't shed it" is increasingly informing social attitudes and family policy.

Healthy families

Creating a healthy social environment means making it possible for the vulnerable – disabled and elderly people, women, and children – to enjoy the same quality of life as everyone else. To achieve this very real possibility, government measures are needed giving these groups full equality in law and access to information, benefits, and services, the right to self-representation, and involvement in all decisions affecting their lives. Channels can also be created enabling them to obtain help from outside the family in cases of victimization and neglect.

To date a great deal has been achieved. In industrialized countries, telephone hotlines, information and advice centres, support groups, and legal aid programmes are all in place. The US is the only country in the world with anti-discrimination laws on disability, passed in 1990, while human rights charters have been established in Canada, Sweden, and some Australian states. Many other countries also have equal opportunities laws. But they are not always implemented.

Empowering disabled people to lead full lives requires extra resources, as do health education and care to prevent the conditions that lead to disability. Planners should recognize the needs of people with disabilities when designing public transport, housing, and other amenities. And educational work to change public attitudes toward disabled people is also vital.

Indifference has meant that assistance and disability grants in many countries are often confined to a few ill-equipped institutions. Even in relatively enlightened countries such as the US and UK disabled people are three times more likely to be unemployed than the able-bodied.

Despite the giant obstacles, progress is possible. The first key step is to recognize and air a problem. Public outcry, fuelled by the media, is a powerful agent for change. When the battered baby syndrome was identified by doctors in the early 1960s it

Self-help is often the only form of support for some family members. For these Nigerian women (above), their agricultural co-operative gives them an income and a little independence.

● In 1985 a police station staffed entirely by women was opened in Sao Paulo, Brazil, to offer help to female victims of violence.

shocked public and professional carers alike. But now that the problem has been identified steps have been taken to guard against it. Western social services are quick to spot the danger signs and act. And where society is slow to act, the disadvantaged are forced to lead the fight.

Self-help groups have proved a huge success. Domestic violence was highlighted by the women's movement which established the first shelter for battered wives in the UK and Canada in 1971. Now there are hundreds of such refuges providing residential support and other services right around the world, from the US and UK to Thailand, Egypt, Trinidad, and Tobago. In 1993 men established their own shelter in London for male victims of domestic violence.

Those deprived of a family's support may also be empowered. About 1000 of London's homeless people sell a twice-monthly magazine, *The Big Issue*, as an alternative to the humiliation of begging. *Street News*, the New York equivalent, sells 150,000 copies a month.

Crediting the poor

The Grameen Bank was started in one Bangladesh village in 1976. Its objective was to give banking facilities to the poorest – the landless poor. About 90% of its loans are to women and by 1990 the bank had grown to 18,500 villages, lending to 800,000 people. More than 90,000 homes have been built with the loans and the default rate is less than 3% a year. The benefits are great: families are far less likely to starve, their homes weather the monsoon, many children have started school, and the poorest are organizing among themselves. The bank has led to similar initiatives in India, Africa, Latin America, and even Arkansas, US.

'**Children are people of equal value.** They must be given a channel through which they can be heard", says Trond Torgensen, the doctor appointed as Norway's children's ombudsman.

Since 1981, Norway has had an official called the "Barneombudet" – the Advocate for Children. This official ensures that "children are seen as people, with their own needs and their own rights". The Barneombudet has the right to comment on policy and to promote the interests of children in both public and private sectors. The Barneombudet has no authority to decide on individual cases, interfere with the legal process of the courts, or change official decisions, but can give an opinion on a case involving a child once judgment has been made.

The Barneombudet's successes are as varied as working with the Norwegian energy ministry to move high-tension wires from where children play, to successfully lobbying for a law to prohibit parental striking of children. A free telephone line has been set up so children can call with their messages about what they think is important, and a weekly television show allows the Barneombudet to follow up children's responses.

It seems that ombudswork for children will soon be active in many more countries: one is currently being established in Costa Rica. How far its powers increase depends on the strength of public support and the tenacity shown by those who are willing to take the initiative for change.

Those who are marginalized in society have responsibilities. Usually they have little say in decisions and procedures affecting them, and little involvement in planning and policy development generally. Since it is widely believed that they are not competent to participate in decision-making they in turn tend to accept that they are powerless, silent, and lacking control over their lives. They end up depending on others to articulate their needs and protect their interests. But that should not be the case.

By forming pressure groups to lobby politicians or mount public campaigns, special interest groups can, and indeed have, become a political force to be reckoned with. A small interesting example occurred in the 1970s. A group of American high school students, having seen many of their peers leave school pregnant, formed a coalition to petition the Board of Education for a programme of sex education. And that initiative led to the hiring of peer counsellors offering information on pregnancy, venereal disease, and referral services.

Even though planners sometimes consult the marginal groups about new services and facilities, the outcome can prove unpredictable. Disabled Peoples' International emerged in 1981 through sheer frustration with traditional clinical approaches to disability and the tendency to ignore disabled people's views. The movement has made independence a priority by fighting for integrated facilities, accessible public transport, and appropriate housing, care, and equipment. It now has affiliate organizations in more than 90 countries, and has set up a research centre in the UK, run by and for disabled people.

Inviting vulnerable groups to participate in designing projects increases the likelihood that new services will match needs and therefore be well used. Children from the Young People's East Harlem Resource Center, New York, were involved in designing a local park. Access, safety, and security were discussed and three-dimensional models were built to show the location of features such as benches and gardens. Extensive use has been made of the facility, and levels of vandalism are exceptionally low.

There have been a number of such initiatives in recent years aimed specifically at involving children in decision-making. Children's participation in the political process is seen by some as an important step in the development of a democratic society. This partly motivated the Voice of the Children Campaign, which has organized children's public hearings in 25 countries. The hearings give children the opportunity to debate

a voice to the silent

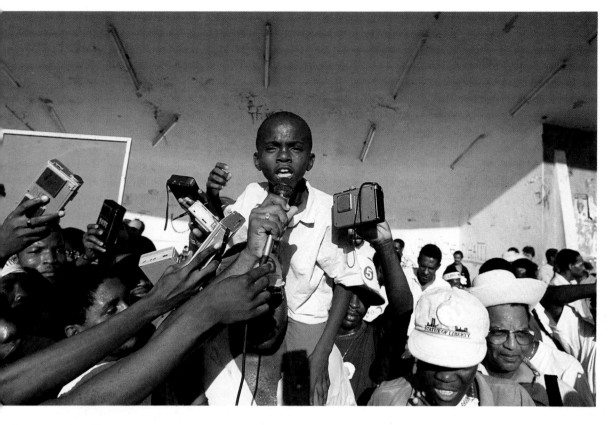

The pioneering Children's Interests Bureau of South Australia campaigns for the rights of young people.
Founded in 1983 and based in Adelaide, it researches subjects affecting child welfare, develops welfare services, and evaluates government policies. It gives advice on how children can be separately represented and ensure their rights are protected in custody or access cases. The bureau also monitors environmental planning to ensure that the needs of children – especially the disabled – are catered for. Its interventionist role is shown by the establishment of advocacy, arbitration, and mediation procedures for children – especially those in state care.

Young teenagers' feelings about decision-making, authority, and discipline is the subject of a recent research project by the bureau. It found, unsurprisingly, that they want to contribute to the decisions affecting their lives. A sequel to this was its publication of a booklet that poses questions most often raised by the young and provides carefully researched, factual answers. A section entitled Legal Guardianship dealing with questions relating to divorce, adoption, and care is followed by questions on punishment and education. Children may ask, for example, "Who can punish me?" The booklet tells them: "Under the age of 18 your parents may give 'moderate and reasonable' corporal punishment. What is reasonable depends on the circumstances – your age and size, what you have done, how hard you were hit, and whether you were injured. If you are injured, your parents/guardians could be charged with an offence."

This Haitian orphan (above) is neither silent nor powerless as he commands attention at a political rally for Father Aristide in 1990.

Do you love us?
A twelve-year-old girl addressed the 1992 Earth Summit. "Parents used to comfort their children by saying 'Everything is going to be alright...it's not the end of the world'. But, you can't say that to us anymore. Our planet is becoming worse for all future children...Are we even on your list of priorities? You grown-ups say you love us, but we challenge you to make your actions reflect your words."

Age brings wisdom and experience in the ways of the world. Youth brings energy and hope. Both are uniquely combined within the family (above).

with political leaders on environmental and development issues such as public transport, the debt crisis, and military spending.

The more special interest groups are given a chance to participate, the more they, and others, realize they can have a powerful and influential voice, and have an opportunity to control their lives.

Listening ears

33 carefully selected, housebound elderly people in Chicago run a telephone advice line for children from 3pm to 6pm daily. Up to 500 calls per month are handled covering subjects from bullying at school to teenage pregnancy.

As new patterns of rights and responsibilities within the family emerge in modern society, so the roles of individual members need reassessing. Conventionally, most responsibility and power has been given to the "breadwinner", or the patriarch. In contrast, those who are not economically independent – the elderly, children, teenagers, and disabled people – have often been seen as burdens on the family. But matters are rapidly improving.

As the populations of many countries age, so an increasing number of families will consist of three or four generations. Instead of seeing people at either end of the age spectrum – the young and the old – as dependent or a burden, society is increasingly recognizing them as an essential family resource.

Devolving rights and responsibilities more equitably to all family members will have two key benefits. It will give dependent, vulnerable groups greater confidence and self-reliance, and enable them to contribute equally with others. And it will reduce the burden of responsibilities on society. In a world of retreating public funds, making better use of the human resources within the family is one of the most important initiatives for family welfare.

In the West, teenagers present a special problem for many families today. Often unable to adjust to their ambiguous status as part-child, part-adult, many face unemployment on leaving school and few are aware of the job opportunities that are available. Breaking down young people's isolation from working environments can contribute to their wellbeing and gradual assumption of responsibility within the family. The family itself can do much by allowing its teenagers to access and understand parental work patterns. Schools and employers can help, too. In some countries the world of work is now part of the school curriculum. In addition to direct work experience, lessons are devoted to careers guidance, training in economic awareness and understanding, and other related topics.

The young have enormous energy; a society which offers them no scope will suffer. In a time of high unemployment, voluntary work is seen by many as an alternative route to adulthood and self-respect, as well as a way of harnessing their energy to benefit the community. This philosophy motivates the Boy Scout and Girl Guide movements globally. In the Yemen and Peru adult literacy campaigns have used thousands of young volunteers from youth clubs and schools. The "Child to Child" programme, devised by the Institute of Child Health in London, acknowledges that children can be an important resource in maintaining family health and welfare. School-age children in countries all over the world are trained as health scouts to detect health and nutrition problems in younger siblings and help their families take preventive measures.

The young – the world's next generation – are one of the family's greatest assets, and if given the chance can greatly improve their own, and other people's lives.

the family resource

Involving the young
Many countries organize schemes involving young people. In 1984 the Democratic Yemen mounted a national adult literacy campaign. More than 20,000 secondary school pupils and members of the Yemeni Youth Organization taught nearly 200,000 men and women to read and write.

epilogue

As the twentieth century draws to a close, human society is challenged by economic, political, and environmental changes more dramatic than ever before. We live in a world defined by change. A world where people live longer in an increasingly adult society; where more families migrate away from their origins and cluster in huge, congested urban centres; where new employment patterns are evolving; where the division of roles between men and women becomes increasingly blurred.

Through all this, the family remains both central and strong. For centuries it has withstood social catastrophes and revolutions – but it has not remained unchanged by them. We are at a crossroads between what the family has been, and what it will become in the future. Childhood, parenthood, old age – all are likely to be redefined. The emergence of a new political class of older people, for example, is just one issue families and governments still have to grapple with. These older people are likely to have the health (and sometimes the wealth) to act as a powerful source of support for family life. As human society becomes more complex, so the great diversity of family lives and forms is expected to continue.

Yet the ideas we have about families that are enshrined in our laws, policies, and media are often out-dated and at odds with

The generation-in waiting (left). "Children begin by loving their parents; as they grow older they judge them; sometimes they forgive them." *Oscar Wilde*

reality. They sometimes work against the grain of change, rather than with it. They accuse increasingly large numbers of people of living in the wrong kinds of families, rather than ensuring that policies are adapted to suit a world in transition – and to cushion the painful effects of change.

We should all recognize that successful family life is neither enforced dependency, nor isolated individualism, but interdependence. Within families, this implies a relationship between equals – gender and generations. Within communities, social institutions should support families enough to empower them, but not trap them in dependency.

If we do not invest in families, we may pay a high price. For most individuals, the family is by far the most significant institution. 'Whether we grow up anxious or confident, trusting or suspicious, ambitious or contented, is determined very largely by our early experiences of family life. For society, the imagined savings of reducing state support for families in their key roles are far outweighed by the resulting costs in addiction, ill health, crime, school drop-out rates, and by callous self-interest. These are evils which a well-supported family and child-hood can reduce or eliminate.

Governments tend to work on short time-scales, restricting their horizons to the term of office. By contrast, families work, and live, on life-long perspectives.

If there were adequate political recognition of the significance of parenting, men could begin to take a greater share in it, and there would be more preparation of the young for this role by bringing it to the fore in their education. A state serious about the family would, as some have proposed, prepare family impact statements for each new law proposed. And governments would appoint high-ranking officials responsible for safeguarding the interests of children and parents. But why stop there? Why are the interests of "the family" not represented internationally, at the United Nations, for instance?

Politicians searching for a "big idea" would do well to recognize that strengthening families, and supporting parents in their most significant role, is an investment in the future of society as a whole. Many social ills plague our society, but these dragons can be slain if we attach priority to our duty for the wellbeing of our children – and their children.

Both protecting and empowering the family is of crucial importance if those future generations are to enjoy a decent quality of life. The family is the most fundamental resource for human society. Guaranteeing the transfer of resources between generations is fundamental to the notion of "sustainability". The present generation has a responsibility to future ones to provide a healthier, more secure environment for the family to act out its central role in human society.

Toward a declaration on the family

The "Guiding Principles on the Family" is a document created by the NGO Committee on the Family based at the UN in Vienna. It reflects the NGO's views about the functions, rights, and responsibilities of the family and represents one idea of the form a UN declaration might take.

Preamble

Society is formed by a plurality of entwined groups and entities and a multitude of individual persons, with their own specific objectives and purposes. Among these groups, families are the basic social unit and are acknowledged to be among their society's fundamental and most important characteristics.

For, in all countries, at all times and in all civilizations, the family, regardless of its form and organization, is recognized as a social reality and as an essential element for development.

The term "family" covers a wide range of structures, types, values and functions. These differ within countries and from region to region. In every society the family is continuously evolving and changes occur as its members pass through the different stages of their life cycle.

The family aims to provide a source of mutual love, respect, solidarity and affection and to act as a support system for the individual rights of its members. Families are the setting where values are transmitted from one generation to another.

Families also play a fundamental role as intermediate bodies between the individual and the state and other social agents.

The family is a powerful agent for social, political, economic and cultural change and a potential vehicle for development. However, the family can also be influenced by the nature and pace of change, which often exerts pressure on families. Such forces can make the family extremely vulnerable and in need of support from other institutions.

Therefore, the family should be granted protection and assistance so that it can fully assume its responsibilities as the basic unit of society, the natural environment for its members, particularly children and youth, and in many cases the only support system for the ageing and the disabled.

For this purpose, policies and appropriate legislation for the promotion and strengthening of families should be a priority concern of national governments and inter-governmental organizations.

The role and contribution of the concerned non-governmental organizations in strengthening the family should be stressed at all levels.

The proclamation of the International Year of the Family 1994 is a consequence of the particular appreciation for the family shown by the United Nations and a proof of its intention to give stronger support to families as the basis of society.

In fact, over the years various United Nations policies and strategies have been formulated which support and strengthen the family unit. One of the earliest statements about families is contained in the Universal Declaration of Human Rights, which states that "the family is the fundamental group unit of society and is entitled to protection by society and the State".

Many other international legal documents repeatedly declare that the family is the basic unit of society and that, as such, it should be protected and assisted by society and the State.

It might, therefore, be desirable to embody all these references to the family in a coherent and detailed declaration on the functions, responsibilities and rights of the family, as one of the objectives of the International Year of the Family 1994, on the understanding that rights already established by the United Nations should in no way be restricted in such a declaration.

Family formation

Article 1

1 The best conditions should be promoted for family formation and family life.
2 The free and full consent of the partners should be secured when entering a union as a basis of a family. A minimum age for entering such a union should be fixed by law.

Respect for all types of families

Article 2

Regional, national and cultural differences in all types of families should be respected and discrimination among them avoided. This respect and non-discrimination should aim at the dignity of the family, the protection of family life and the full development of individual family members.

Article 3

Respect should be shown for the religious, philosophical and ethical values or political opinions of each family member and for his or her freedom to manifest, as a family or in community with others, their culture and religion.

Autonomy and support of family functions

Article 4

All families have the right and the responsibility to freely organize their internal functioning, taking into account the best interest of each of their members.

Article 5

1 Legislation which has a direct bearing on the welfare of families and their members should be flexible and periodically reviewed and adapted to the changing social, cultural and economic conditions, in particular with a view to the concept of equality between women and men.
2 Social welfare programmes and activities should be designed to strengthen and revitalize families in their functions.
3 All policies, at national and international levels, in developing as well as in industrialized countries, should take into account their impact on families.

Family needs

Article 6

It should be recognized that families need an adequate standard of living to meet their basic human needs and for the physical, spiritual, ethical, cultural and social development of their members and as a family.

Article 7

The special needs of disadvantaged families should be addressed and help given to them to overcome their adversity. The following should receive special economic and social protection:
• Disadvantaged families in rural and poor urban areas;
• Families confronted with special problems – e.g. disabled members, inability to obtain gainful employment, low income, dependent ageing members, large families and single parent families;
• Young people taking up family responsibilities;
• Families affected by war and environmental disasters, and for political and economic reasons.

Parenthood

Article 8

1 Parents have the basic right to determine freely and responsibly the number and spacing of their children as well as to have access to the knowledge and means necessary to enable them to exercise this right.
2 Family-planning programmes should direct information and services towards men and women alike, to ensure responsible parenthood, mutual respect, understanding and co-operation.
3 Reproductive, pre- and post-natal care should be strengthened within social and health systems.

Article 9

1 Parental leave regulations should address both mothers and fathers, since recent research discloses the important role fathers are playing in the socialization of their children. Therefore, special efforts should be made to enhance the role of fathers, thus ensuring at the same time equality between both parents.
2 Appropriate maternity leave, social and financial support should be made available to all mothers, employed or not.
3 Adequate child-care facilities should be provided in the interest of family life.

The child

Article 10

1 All children shall enjoy the same social protection and rights and be given equal opportunities to develop their full potential.
2 All children should have fair chances to grow up in a family environment. In case they are deprived of their family

environment, they shall be entitled to special protection and assistance.
3 Whenever a legal guardian or tutor needs to be established for a family member, legal authorities should consider the eligibility of another member of the same family as a matter of priority.

Responsibilities of parents
Article 11

1 Parents share the primary responsibility for bringing up their children and providing them with an adequate standard of living.
2 The right and responsibility of parents to provide guidance appropriate to the child's evolving capacities should be respected, without infringing on the child's right to freedom of thought, conscience and expression.

Education
Article 12

1 The family shall respect and foster the right of each of its members, especially girls and women, to receive formal education and continuous education. This education shall be free and compulsory at least in the elementary and fundamental stages.
2 Young people of both sexes should receive special preparation for responsible family and sexual life and parenthood as well as adequate education for managing the resources necessary for everyday life.
3 Parents have the responsibility to continuously educate and improve themselves and to instil in their children the values of mutual respect and understanding and a sense of responsibility for the environment and sustainable development. In this they should be supported by the educational system, the media and other networks.

Intra-family relations and roles
Article 13

1 To be a member of a family implies communication and solidarity with other family members and mutual responsibility. Within the family unit, joint decision-making should be encouraged. The more-able members should endeavour to support the less-able ones, when these are impaired by age, infirmity or other forms of hardship.
2 Full development of each individual family member is necessary for the exercise of his/her rights and responsibilities within and outside the family, as well as for the family's welfare.
3 Major attention should be given to equal rights and equal responsibilities for men and women within the family, including equitable sharing of roles and tasks in the household.

Harmonizing family life and work
Article 14

1 The family members and the family as a group are entitled to free time, rest and family life.

2 Policies and programmes should be developed to enable family members to harmonize activities of professional life with family life.
3 Unpaid work inside and outside the family – e.g. household activities, food production at the family level, social and voluntary work – have generally been perceived as having low economic and social prestige. All societies should place a higher value on these activities by including them in the GNP (gross national product), in official statistical data and by providing certain corresponding forms of social security.

Violence and neglect
Article 15

1 All efforts should be made to prevent violence, neglect, abuse and exploitation within the family and to raise public awareness of such hidden crimes. Legislation and other measures should be enacted and implemented in order to eradicate this violence and protect the victims.
2 The full physical and mental integrity of young girls and boys is a prerequisite to enable them to develop into mature and responsible adults. Therefore, all kinds of mutilations should be forbidden.
3 Measures should be provided by public authorities to eliminate social conditions leading to drug and alcohol addiction and to all forms of violence, such as vandalism, delinquency, aggression and crime. Help and rehabilitation should be made available to families confronted with such problems.

Family counselling
Article 16

1 All efforts should be made to establish a well organized network of family counselling services, inter alia to provide educational, psychological and social assistance.
2 Adequate training is essential for those who may become responsible for family counselling.
3 Even though the courts of justice should be the ultimate recourse for legal aid, it is indispensable that the magistrates of these courts are also adequately trained.

Consumer protection
Article 17

All legal measures or policies should be adopted to protect the family against unsafe and unhealthy goods, mislabelling and unethical and exploitative marketing practices.

Tax liability
Article 18

Any tax system should encourage family solidarity and help to ensure the family's minimum standard of living.

Association and participation
Article 19

The Declaration of Human Rights entitles individuals to create associations. Hence,

families are entitled to establish associations and enjoy freedom of public and private assembly.

Mass communications media
Article 20

Given the great potential of the mass-media as a vehicle for social change, every effort should be made to have the media exercise a positive, educative and respectful attitude regarding the family and family life.

Peace and security
Article 21

1 Peace and security are a prerequisite for a healthy environment, sustainable development and for social and economic progress for the benefit of all and particularly the family.
2 To this end, resources should be progressively channelled from military to social programmes.
3 All feasible measures shall be taken to ensure that persons below the age of 18 do not take a direct part in armed conflicts.

bibliography

Abbott, M, *Family Ties,* Routledge, New York, 1993

Bohannon, P and Middletone, J, *Kinship and Social Organization,* Natural History Press, New York, 1968

Boyden, J and Holden, P, *Children of the Cities,* Zed Books, London, 1991

Brown, L R et al., *State of the World 1992,* Earthscan, London, and W W Norton, New York, 1992

Brown, L R et al., *State of the World 1993,* Earthscan, London, and W W Norton, New York, 1992

Brown, L R, Flavin, C, and Kane, H, *Vital Signs 1992,* Earthscan, London, and W W Norton, New York, 1992

Casey, J, *The History of the Family,* Blackwell, Oxford, 1989

Centre for Social Development and Humanitarian Affairs, *Social Support Mechanisms for the Advancement of Women, Women 2000 No. 3,* United Nations Office at Vienna, 1988

Centre for Social Development and Humanitarian Affairs, *Violence against Women in the Family,* UN, New York, 1989

Cornia, G A, *Child Poverty and Deprivation in Industrialized Countries,* Innocenti Occasional Papers No. 2, Florence, 1990

Coote, A, Harman, H, and Hewitt, P, *The Family Way: A New Approach to Policy-Making, Social Policy Paper No. 1,* PPR, London, 1990

Department of International Economic and Social Affairs, *The Family: Models for Providing Comprehensive Services for Family and Child Welfare,* UN, New York, 1984

Danziger, S, and Stern, J, *The Causes and Consequences of Child Poverty in the United States,* Innocenti Occasional Papers No. 10, Florence, 1990

Ekins, P, Hillman, M, and Hutchison, R, *Wealth Beyond Measure,* Gaia Books, London, 1992, and Green Economics, Doubleday, New York, 1992

Fyfe, A, *Child Labour,* Polity Press, Cambridge, 1989

Girardet, H, *The Gaia Atlas of Cities,* Gaia Books, London, and Doubleday, New York, 1992

Goldsmith, J, *Childbirth Wisdom: From the World's Oldest Societies,* East West Health Books, USA, 1990

Goody, J, *The Development of the Family and Marriage in Europe,* Cambridge University Press, Cambridge, 1983

Hartmann, B, *Reproductive Rights and Wrongs,* Harper and Row, New York, 1987

Held, D (ed), *States and Societies,* Basil Blackwell, Oxford, 1983

International Social Science Journal, *Changing Family Patterns,* No 126, Blackwell, Oxford, 1990

Jones, C, *Patterns of Social Policy,* Tavistock Publications, London, 1985

Kitzinger, S, *Ourselves as Mothers: The Universal Experience of Motherhood,* Doubleday, London, 1992

Korbin, J L (ed), *Child Abuse and Neglect,* University of California Press, Berkeley, 1981

Long, N (ed), *Family and Work in Rural Societies,* Tavistock Publications, New York, 1984

MacCormack, C and Strathern, M (eds), *Nature, Culture and Gender,* Cambridge University Press, Cambridge 1980

MacPherson, S, *Five Hundred Million Children: Poverty and Child Welfare in the Third World,* Wheatsheaf Books, Hemel Hempstead, UK, 1987

Maybury-Lewis, D, *Millennium: Tribal Wisdom and the Modern World,* Viking Penguin, New York, 1992

McCredie, G and Horrox, A, *Voices in the Dark: Children and Divorce,* Unwin Paperbacks, London, 1985

McLoughlin, J, *The Demographic Revolution,* Faber, London, 1991

Miles, R, *The Women's History of the World,* Grafton Books, London, 1988

Myers, N (ed), *Gaia: An Atlas of Planet Management,* Pan, London, 1985, and Doubleday, New York, 1993

Myers, R, *The Twelve Who Survive,* Routledge, London, 1992

NGO Committee on the Family, *Family: A Topic for International Debate and Action,* UN Office at Vienna, 1991

Robertson, A F, *Beyond the Family: The Social Organization of Human Reproduction,* Polity Press, Cambridge, 1991

Seel, R, *The Uncertain Father: Exploring Modern Fatherhood,* Gateway Books, Bath, UK, 1987

Sivard, R L, *World Military and Social Expenditures 1991,* World Priorities Inc., Washington DC, 1991

Taylor, D, *Women: A World Report,* Methuen, London, 1985

Timberlake, L and Thomas, L, *When the Bough Breaks,* Earthscan, London, 1990

UNICEF, *The State of the World's Children 1992,* Oxford University Press, London and New York, 1992

United Nations, *The World's Women 1970–1990: Trends and Statistics,* UN, New York, 1991

United Nations Development Programme, *Human Development Report 1992,* Oxford University Press, Oxford and New York, 1992

Waring, M, *If Women Counted,* Macmillan, London, 1988

White, D and Woollett, A, *Families: A Context for Development,* The Falmer Press, London, 1992

World Health Organization, *Global Status of Reproductive Health,* WHO, Geneva, 1992

Zelizer, V A, *Pricing the Priceless Child: The Changing Social Value of Children,* Basic Books Inc., USA, 1985

Support Groups and Helplines

Childline
Freepost 1111
London EC4B 4BB
tel: 0800 1111

Contact A Family
*supporting families with children
who have special needs*
16 Strutton Ground
London SW1P 2HP
tel: 071 222 2695

Exploring Parenthood
Latimer Education Centre
194 Freston Road
London W10 6TT
tel: 081 960 1678

Families Need Fathers
134 Curzon Road
London EC2A 3AR
tel: 071 613 5060

Gingerbread (England and Wales)
support for single parents
35 Wellington Street
London WC2E 7BN
tel: 071 240 0953

Gingerbread (Scotland)
Community Central Hall
304 Maryhill Road
Glasgow G20 7YA
tel: 041 353 0989

National Council for One
Parent Families
255 Kentish Town Road
London NW5 2LX
tel: 071 267 1361

The Parent Network
44-46 Caversham Road
London NW5 2DS
tel: 071 485 8535

Parents' Anonymous
6 Manor Gardens
London N7 6LA
tel: 081 668 4805

Relate
Herbert Gray College
Little Church Street
Rugby CV21 3AP
tel: 0788 573241

Single Parent Action Network
14 Robertson Road
Bristol BS5 6JY
tel: 0272 514231

Women's Aid Federation
*Refuge network offering support
or temporary safety to women
and children who have suffered
domestic abuse*
England tel: 0272 633542
Scotland tel: 031 225 8011
Wales tel: 0222 390874

Social Development

ActionAid
Tapstone Road
Chard TA20 2AB

Action on Disability and
Development
23 Lower Keyford
Frome BA11 4AP

HelpAge International
St James's Walk
London EC1R 0BE

International Planned
Parenthood Federation
Regent's College
Inner Circle
Regent's Park
London NW1 4NS

OXFAM
274 Banbury Road
Oxford OX2 7DZ

Panos Institute
9 White Lion Street
London N1 9PD

Quaker Peace and Service
Religious Society of Friends
Friends House
Euston Road
London NW1 2BJ

Save the Children Fund
17 Grove Lane
London SE5 8RD

United Nations High Commissioner
for Refugees (UNHCR) UK
7 Westminster Palace Gardens
Artillery Row
London SW1P 1R

United Nations Children's Fund
(UNICEF) UK
55 Lincoln's Inn Fields
London WC2A 3NB

Womankind (Worldwide)
122 Whitechapel High Street
London E1 7PT

World Development Movement
25 Beehive Place
London SW9 7QR

Y-Care International
640 Forest Road
London E17 3DZ

Human Rights

Amnesty International British Section
99-119 Rosebery Avenue
London EC1R 4RE

Childhope UK
40 Rosebery Avenue
London EC1R 4RN

Children's Legal Centre
20 Compton Terrace
London N1 2UN

Children's Rights Development Unit
235 Shaftesbury Avenue
London WC2H 8EL

Disabled Peoples' International
11 Belgrave Road
London SW1V 1RS

Minority Rights Group
379 Brixton Road
London SW9 7DE

Family Research

Family Policy Studies Centre
231 Baker Street
London NW1 6XE

Institute for Public Policy Research
18 Buckingham Gate
London SW1E 6LB

Institute of Family Therapy
43 New Cavendish Street
London W1M 7RG

Environment

Global Action Plan UK
PO Box 893
London E5 9RU

Parents for Safe Food
5-11 Worship Street
London EC2 2BH

Women's Environment Network
Aberbeen Studios
22 Highbury Grove
London N5 2EA

organizations

International

Bernard Van Leer Foundation
PO Box 82334
2508 EH
The Hague
Netherlands

Caritas Internationalis
Palazzo San Calisto
00120 Cité du Vatican

Confederation of Family
Organizations in the EC
17 rue de Londres
1050 Brussels
Belgium

Defence for Children International
PO Box 88
1211 Geneva 20
Switzerland

Family Care International
588 Broadway
Suite 510
New York
NY 10012
USA

International Association of Juvenile
and Family Court Magistrates
Palais de Justice
75055 Paris
France

International Catholic Child Bureau
65 rue de Lausanne
1202 Geneva
Switzerland

International Council of Women
13 rue Caumartin
75009 Paris
France

International Movement ATD
Fourth World
107 avenue du Général Leclerc
95480 Pierrelaye
France

International Society for the
Prevention of Child Abuse
and Neglect
Achtergracht 29
1017 WM Amsterdam
Netherlands

International Union of Family
Organizations
28 place St-Georges
75009 Paris
France

League of Red Cross and
Red Crescent Societies
17 Chemin des Crêts
BP 372
1211 Geneva 19
Switzerland

Mother and Child International
Kürbergstrasse 1
8049 Zurich
Switzerland

Quaker Peace and Service
Quaker UN Office
13 avenue du Mervelet
1209 Geneva
Switzerland

Secretariat for the International
Year of the Family
United Nations Office at Vienna
PO Box 500
1400 Vienna
Austria

United Nations Centre for
Human Rights
8-14 avenue de la Paix
1211 Geneva 10
Switzerland

United Nations Children's Fund
(UNICEF)
3 United Nations Plaza
New York
NY 10017
USA

United Nations Development
Programme (UNDP)
1 UN Plaza
New York
NY 10017
USA

United Nations Division for the
Advancement of Women
United Nations Office at Vienna
PO Box 500
1400 Vienna
Austria

United Nations Educational,
Scientific and Cultural Organization
(UNESCO)
7 Place de Fontenoy
75700 Paris
France

United Nations High Commission
for Refugees (UNHCR)
PO Box 2500
1211 Geneva 2
Switzerland

United Nations Population Fund
(UNFPA)
220 East 42nd Street
New York
NY 10017
USA

University for Peace
PO Box 138
Ciudad Colón
Costa Rica
Central America

Voice of the Children
Northern Secretariat
Langes gate 4
0165 Oslo 1
Norway

Voice of the Children
Southern Secretariat
Casilla de Correo 83
Correo Central
5000 Cordoba
Argentina

World Health Organization (WHO)
1211 Geneva 27
Switzerland

index

index

Author's acknowledgements

While I enjoyed tackling such an ambitious project and must bear the major responsibility for the outcome, this book is the result of teamwork and there are a number of people who contributed to its creation to whom I am extremely grateful. Maggie Black wrote several important sections in parts three and four, read much of the text in draft, and made many useful and provocative comments. Wendy Davies assembled lively case studies to punctuate the text. Philip Parker was my patient and conscientious editor, who in addition to spending many weeks working on the text, provided a constant flow of reflective thought and new information. Lucy Guenot, the designer of this volume, successfully matched images to ideas. Sally Crawford gave me some fascinating historical leads on the Anglo saxon Family. Brian Pratt read the various drafts, made numerous suggestions, and gave me many ideas. Finally, my own family - two daughters and sons, their father, grandparents, and nanny - have shown great forebearance and given the huge degree of support usually only found within the network of kin. I dedicate this book to them.

Publisher's acknowledgements

Gaia Books warmly thanks all those who have contributed to the birth of this book. Deep thanks go to Jo Boyden, Maggie Black, and Wendy Davies for writing to a tight schedule. And we are especially indebted to Sir Peter Ustinov for his thought-provoking introduction. At UNESCO, we thank Dr Federico Mayor for his Foreword, and John Bennett, Chief of the Young Child in Family Environment Project, for his unstinting faith in the book and constructive comments, from first synopsis to final text. Equally, we thank Robert Myers for his essential review of the text, and Henryk Sokalski, Co-ordinator of the International Year of the Family, for his support and comments. Gaia also thanks: Michelle Atkinson for energy-efficient organization; Kitty Parker-Jervis for design assistance; Natasha Goddard, Mme Tioulong-Farras, Caroline Sheldrick, and Richard Rosenfeld for help at the final hurdle; Susan Walby for production: Nan Wise and Suzy Boston for liaison; and Mary Warren for indexing.

Photographic credits

Abbreviations: t = top, b = bottom, l = left, r = right, tl = top left, etc.
Action on Disability and Development: (Cheryl A Koralik) p.37
Common Cause: (Simon Grossett) p.88 (tl)
The Daily Telegraph: (Peter Sandground) p.139
Format: (Sue Darlow) p.82 (bl); (Judy Harrison) p. 78; (Jenny Matthews) p.57, p.151; (Maggie Murray) p.26, p.30
The Guardian: (M Bunting) p.51
Robert Harding Picture Library: (Yoram Lehmann) pp.40-1; (J H C Wilson) p.88 (tr)
The Hutchison Library: p.35 (t), p.42 (bl), p.46, p.82 (t); (Sarah Errington) p.32; (Jeremy A. Horner) p.35 (br)
Impact: (Michael George) pp.132-3; (Caroline Penn) p.136
MSM International Ltd: (Gotz Liuzenmeier) p.105
Magnum: (Abbas) pp.20-1; (Micha Baram) p.58-9 (t); (Bruno Barbey) p.142, p.77; (R Branco) pp.108-9; (Jean Gaumy) p.146 (tl); (Peter Marlow) pp. 88-9 (b); (Steve McCurry) pp. 66-7, p.100; (James Nachtwey) p. 124; (John Nance) p.16; (Michael K Nichols) p.13, pp.14-5, p.25, p.80; (Chris Steele Perkins) p.54, p.66 (b), p.106, pp.140-1; (Raghu Rai) p.10, p.64; (Eugene Richards) p.62, p.128; (Sebastiao Salgado) p.160; (Alex Webb) p.111 (bl)
Network: (Mike Abrahams) p.94; (Hans J Burkard) pp.22-3 pp.110-1 (b); (Mike Goldwater) pp.18-9, p.87; (Robert Hutchings) p.75; (Stephen Shames Matrix) p.96; (Jenny Matthews) p.42-3 (t), p.118, pp.146-7 (b); (Martin Mayer) p.97; (Gideon Mendel) p.123; (C Pillitz) pp.2-3; (J Sturrock) p.116; (Homer Sykes) p.58 (b)
Christine Osborne Pictures: p.158
Oxfam: (Bernard Broughton) p.148
Panos Pictures: pp.154-5; (Marc French) p.157; (Penny Tweedie) p.152
Mary Roberts: pp.28-9
Iain Stewart: p.60
Survival International: (Victor Englebert) pp.38-9
UNESCO: (Dominique Roger) p.6

acknowledgements

Other titles from Gaia Books:

Wealth Beyond Measure
An Atlas of New Economics
by Paul Ekins, Mayer Hillman, and Robert Hutchison
ISBN 1 85675 050 7

*This title explores, describes, and sets out what needs to be done by governments and
people to create prosperity and a fairer world in a healthy environment.*

•

The Gaia Atlas of Cities
New directions for sustainable living
by Herbert Girardet
ISBN 1 85675 065 5

*This is a vital source book of innovative ideas and strategies for making our cities
ecologically sustainable, aiming to generate discussion of new ways of living
and managing our lives in cities.*

•

The Gaia Rainforest Theatre
An educational forest-saving activity for children of all ages, from 7 to 70
Designed by Rick Miller with Gaia Books
ISBN 1 85675 080 9

*The Gaia Rainforest Theatre is a unique concept: a pack consisting of a stunning pull-
out theatre, exotic plants to position yourself, and 19 rainforest characters – from big cats
and birds to insects and humans – to populate the stage.
Three exciting playscript bring the rainforest to life.*

•

Created by Gaia Books and published by Pan Books:

The Gaia Atlas of Planet Management
For today's caretakers of tomorrow's world
General editor: Norman Myers
ISBN 0 330 28491 6

*The touchstone of environmental publishing and possibly the most influential book
in the area. No other work has approached the subject with such visual impact,
passion, or authority. Regularly featured in lists of the top ten books on the environment
ever created, it has been read by millions around the world.*

Contents

Any words appearing in the text in bold, **like this**, are explained in the Glossary.

What is a freshwater fish?

Fish live in different types of water all over the world. Saltwater fish live in salt water, such as the ocean. Freshwater fish live in water that is not salty. There are many types of freshwater **environment**, such as rivers, ponds, and lakes.

This is a **habitat** for wild freshwater fish.

Different environments

All fish are **cold-blooded**. This means they cannot control their own body temperature. Their blood will be the same temperature as the water they swim in. Some fish can live in colder water than others. Some people keep pet fish outside in ponds. These fish can get very cold without dying. This book is about keeping pet fish inside in fish tanks. Some people heat their tanks, so they can keep fish from **tropical**, or warm, environments.

KEEPING PETS

eshwater Fish

Tristan Boyer Binns

www.heinemann.co.uk/library
Visit our website to find out more information about Heinemann Library books.

To order:
 Phone 44 (0) 1865 888066
 Send a fax to 44 (0) 1865 314091
📟 Visit the Heinemann bookshop at www.heinemann.co.uk/library to browse our catalogue and order online.

First published in Great Britain by
Heinemann Library, Halley Court, Jordan Hill,
Oxford OX2 8EJ, part of Harcourt Education.

Heinemann is a registered trademark of
Harcourt Education Ltd.

Editorial: Andrew Farrow and Stig Vatland
Design: Richard Parker and Q2A Solutions
Illustrations: Jeff Edwards
Picture Research: Melissa Allison and
Virginia Stroud-Lewis
Production: Chloe Bloom

Originated by Modern Age Repro
Printed and Bound in China
by South China Printing Company

10 digit ISBN: 0 431 12426 4 (hardback)
13 digit ISBN: 978 0 431 12426 1

10 digit ISBN: 0 431 12453 1 (paperback)
13 digit ISBN: 978 0 431 12453 7

10 09 08 07 06
10 9 8 7 6 5 4 3 2 1

**British Library Cataloguing in Publication
Data**
Binns, Tristan Boyer
Freshwater fish. - (Keeping pets)
1.Freshwater fishes - Juvenile literature
2.Aquarium fishes
639.3'4

A full catalogue record for this book is available
from the British Library.

Acknowledgements
The publishers would like to thank the following
for permission to reproduce photographs: Alamy
Images pp. **9 top** (Greenshoots Communications),
17 left middle (Maximilian Weinzierl); Ardea
pp. **7** (A. E. Bomford), 4 (Andrea Florence); Bruce
Coleman USA p. **24**; Corbis p. **15** Martin Harvey;
DK Images pp. **5, 6 right, 10 left, 35**; FLPA pp. **8**
(Foto Natura Stock), **14** (Wil Meinderts/Foto
Natura); Harcourt Education Ltd (Tudor
Photography) pp. **9 inset, 10 right, 11, 12, 13,
19 bottom, 19 top, 20, 21 left, 21 right, 23,
25 left, 25 right, 26, 27, 28 bottom, 28 top,
30, 31, 32 left, 32 right, 34, 36 left, 36 right,
37, 39 middle, 41 bottom, 45 bottom, 45 top**;
Heather Angel p. **41 top** (Natural Visions);
Oxford Scientific Films p. **6 left**; PhotoEdit p. **19
bottom inset**; Photolibrary.com p. **42** (IPS Co
Ltd); Photomax pp. **17 top, 17 bottom, 17
right middle, 22, 29 bottom, 29 middle, 29
top, 33, 38, 39 bottom, 40, 43**.

Cover photograph reproduced with permission of
NHPA (Joe Blossom).

Different fish

Fish make great pets. They are fun to watch and interesting to learn about. Saltwater fish are harder to keep. You have to control the amount of salt in the water, and the fish are more sensitive. Most beginners start with freshwater fish.

This fish tank has been carefully designed to be like the fish's natural environment.

Need to know

- Keeping pets is a big responsibility. You must keep them healthy and look after them properly.
- If you do not look after them properly, you are making them suffer and breaking the law.
- Before you get any kind of pet, even a goldfish, make sure you will be able to care for it properly.
- You must always ask permission before you buy any pet, and you should go to the shop with an adult who can help you.

Freshwater fish facts

The best way to learn how to care for your pet fish is to learn how they live in the wild. Fish have been around for millions of years. Over time they have **adapted** to where they live. Choose fish that come from a similar **habitat**. They will need the same types of water and temperature.

Finding a level

Some fish swim near the surface of the water. Other fish swim in the middle or at the bottom. Each type has a different shaped mouth. Surface feeders have mouths that point upwards, to gather food at the top of the water. Middle feeders have mouths that point straight ahead, since their food is usually right in front of them. Bottom feeders have mouths that point downwards to suck food off the bottom.

You can see how this fish's mouth has adapted to suit where it swims. Since it lives near the surface, its mouth angles upwards to help it scoop up food easily.

In this tank, as in the wild, some of the fish swim at the top, some in the middle, and some at the bottom.

Having babies

Some fish give birth to live babies, called **fry**, but most fish lay eggs. Some eggs are attached to plants or left to float free. Others are protected in bubble nests and guarded by the parents. Some parents keep the eggs in their mouths until they are ready to hatch. Others have left by the time their babies are born. Some do not seem to know their own babies and may eat them if they are hungry!

Most fish have many babies at once. A lot of the eggs or fry may be eaten by other fish, or the young fish may not find enough food to survive. Having a lot of young is a way of making sure that some babies will survive to be adults.

This fish holds its eggs in its mouth until they hatch, then the babies swim right out!

Help with your hobby

As you get more experienced, you may want to set up and keep specialized tanks. Luckily, many experienced fish keepers like to help beginners. You can find discussion boards, clubs, and societies where experts will help you learn more about your hobby. Look on page 47 for contact information.

Parts of a fish

Freshwater fish may come in many shapes and colours, but their bodies work in the same way.

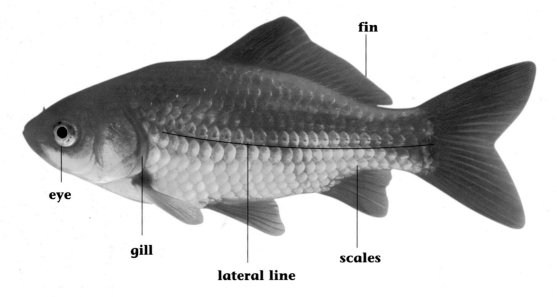

These are some of the important parts of a fish.
- The fins help the fish move. Some fins help it balance.
- Gills work like lungs to bring **oxygen** into the fish.
- The swim bladder is filled with gas. It works like a balloon to keep the fish at the right depth in the water.
- Scales cover the fish. They are like slippery, smooth plates that help it slide easily through the water.
- Nostrils help the fish smell and find food. Fish have different numbers of nostrils in different places.
- A fish's eyes are usually on either side of its head. They let the fish see almost the whole way around it.
- The lateral line is a line of pits that run along a fish's sides. Water fills the pits. As vibrations move through the water, the fish senses them. The lateral line lets the fish sense what is going on all around it.
- The skin of a fish can sense small changes in water temperature. The skin can also feel things that touch it.
- Most fish have **taste buds** in unusual places – on their heads, lips, lining their mouths, on their barbels (like whiskers). Some fish even have taste buds on their fins!

These fish are being farmed in Malaysia. They will be sent all over the world for people to enjoy in their fish tanks and ponds.

Did you know?

Collecting and breeding fish for pets is big business. But in some countries, collecting or breeding fish is harming the **environment**. There are laws to keep animals and their wild **habitats** protected. There is a special award that an international group called the Marine Aquarium Council gives to people who collect or breed fish safely.

Many fish travel a long way before they reach the tanks in a pet shop.

9

Are fish for you?

Fish live in water, not air. Their lives are very different from ours. This makes them interesting to watch as they swim and eat. You can learn about their natural **habitats**, how their bodies work, and what keeps them healthy.

Some people start with a couple of goldfish and become experts as they set up more and more challenging tanks. Who knows, you may become an expert yourself!

The whole family can enjoy watching your pets and learning about their lives.

Ask an adult to help you set up a new tank. You can learn about fish and their **environments** together.

Yes or no?

You need to think about the responsibility that you are taking on before you decide to keep fish. If you do not look after your fish well, they will die. Fish get **stressed** easily. Big changes in temperature, loud noises, and things banging the tank can hurt them. Your whole family has to agree where the tank will go, and understand how to keep your fish calm and happy.

Freshwater fish good points

- It is interesting to watch and learn about them.
- They can live for a long time.
- Once you get into a routine, caring for them is not difficult.
- Fish are quiet pets.
- If you or people in your family are **allergic** to fur or feathers, fish are excellent pets!

Freshwater fish not-so-good points

- Setting up a tank and buying fish can be expensive.
- Fish can get illnesses that can be hard to treat.
- If fish get ill, they need to be **isolated** in a hospital tank.
- Fish do not get to know you and are not cuddly the way other pets are.
- Sometimes fish will **breed**. This can be great, unless you get too many fish! Ask your local fish store for advice.

Caring for fish also means cleaning up after them!

Choosing a tank and fish

Congratulations on deciding to keep fish! Now you need to decide if you will heat the water in your tank so you can keep **tropical** fish. Otherwise you could keep goldfish, which are coldwater fish and do not need a heater.

Setting up your tank

Your fish tank needs to be somewhere light, but not in direct sunlight. It should not be close to a radiator or other source of heat. It should be in a room that stays about the same temperature day and night, all year. Fish like peace and quiet, so a busy hallway would not be a good choice. You also need electricity sockets nearby.

Fish need **oxygen** to breathe. Oxygen gets into the water where the water touches the air in the room. The best fish tanks are not very deep, with a wide, long top opening where the water meets the air. This means plenty of oxygen can reach your fish.

Tanks come in many shapes and sizes. You should be able to find a tank to fit the space you have at home.

On a shelf?

Most fish tanks are too big and heavy to sit on a shelf. You might need a stand for your tank. You will also need somewhere to store all the food, spare parts, nets, and other things your fish will need. A tank stand with a cupboard underneath may be a good choice.

When you buy fish, the dealer puts them in a clear plastic bag inside a paper bag. If it is very hot or cold outside, put the bag inside a **cool box**.

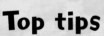

Top tips

- Try to get your fish somewhere local, so the water will not be very different. Very different water can make fish **stressed**.
- The shorter the journey home, the less stressed the fish will get on the way.
- Ask local experts and friends which dealer they buy from. Visit the fish supply shop and check that the fish look healthy, the water looks clear, and the staff are happy to answer your questions.

Choosing fish

Now that you have sorted out your tank, you can choose your fish. You need to work out how many fish will live happily in your tank. First, find out how many litres of water your tank holds. You then decide how many fish you can have by their length when they are fully grown. For each litre (1/4 gallon) of water, you can have about 6 mm (1/6 inch) of fish length. So in a 60 litre (15 gallon) tank, you will have enough room for about 360 mm (14 inches) of fish. A 60 litre (15 gallon) tank is about 60 x 30 x 30 cm (24 x 12 x 12 inches) big.

Special needs

Each type of fish needs certain things to keep it healthy. It may like to swim at the top, middle, or bottom of the tank. It may like very still water or moving water. It may want to be the only one of its type in your tank, have one friend, or swim in a **school** of six or more. It may want to eat other, smaller fish! Make sure you know exactly what each fish is like and what it needs.

Goldfish are great pets. Standard goldfish, like this one, can live a long time and grow very big.

Healthy fish

A healthy fish should swim with its fins out and body the right way up. It should be in the part of the tank it usually likes. It should be interested in food. There should be no spots or fuzzy **fungus** on its body. None of the fins should be torn or ragged. Finally, it should have clear eyes that do not bulge out.

Did you know?

Fish get frightened and **stressed** easily. A stressed fish is more likely to get ill. Keep your fish stress-free by avoiding these things:

- loud noises
- too much activity outside the tank
- overcrowding
- overfeeding
- changes in temperature
- dirty water
- the wrong kind of water
- too much or not enough light
- being moved.

Fancy goldfish can be very interesting to watch! They often have larger bodies and longer fins than common goldfish.

Setting up

At first, it is best to plan on keeping inexpensive, common fish. As you get more experienced, you can keep more unusual types. If you have a heated **tropical** tank, you can choose many different types of fish. Make a final list, but do not buy any fish yet!

Spend time looking through books and visit your fish supply shop, and see what you like. Ask what other fish live happily with the fish you like, and how many you should plan to buy. Make sure the fish you like eat food you can get easily. Make sure you choose fish that swim in all the different levels of the tank.

Settling the tank

You will need to set up the tank and let it settle for about a week before you add any fish. When it has settled, you can add one or two hardy fish. Then you must wait for the water to balance before adding any more (see page 24).

Tropical tank set-up

If you have a 60-litre (15 gallon) tank and keep the temperature between 22 and 26°C (72 to 79°F), you could keep the following group of fish. Add the tetras last, since they are the fussiest about the water.

- Six Neon Tetras – these swim in a group, called a **school**, in the middle of the tank.
- Six Penguin Tetras – these are also called Hockey Sticks, since their stripe looks like a hockey stick. They swim in a school in the middle of the tank.
- Two Dwarf Gourami – they swim in the top to middle of the tank.
- Two Corydoras – they eat food from the bottom.
- Two Swordtails – they swim in the top to middle of the tank.

Another tank setup

This group of fish would live happily in a tank together, kept between 22 and 24°C (72 to 75°F).

This is a Corydoras gossei. It is fine to keep just one. They swim at the bottom.

This is the Lace or Pearl Gourami. You will need two of them. They swim in the middle to upper level.

This is a Fancy Guppy. They like to live in pairs. They swim at the middle level.

This is a Siamese Flying Fox. You will need two. They swim in the middle to bottom level.

What do I need?

To set up a new **aquarium**, you need a lot of things. Before you buy anything, decide which fish you want. Then draw up a tank plan. Since you will have already decided where the tank will go in your home, you can draw its shape and size. Find out what types of plants and hiding places the fish you have chosen need to stay happy. Wood, rocks, and clay flowerpots will look good in your tank. Add your choices to your tank plan.

water

rocks

gravel

tall aquatic plants

wood

small aquatic plants

Before you buy anything, make sure you are happy with your tank plan.

Plug it in

Next, decide on the **filter**, heater, and **hood**. Most beginners use a simple internal sponge filter that is easy to keep clean. Some people prefer an external filter. This hangs outside the tank and sends filtered water back into the tank through a tube. Talk to your fish dealer about what is best for you. To get enough **oxygen** into the tank, many people use an **air rock** as well. These send up a stream of air bubbles that are nice to look at. Some shops sell plastic toys, such as treasure chests, that make bubbles.

If you are setting up a **tropical** tank, you need a heater as well. All tanks need a hood to protect the top and hold the light in place. Most tanks can be bought with a hood and light that fits them perfectly.

Top tip

You need to be very careful with all the electric parts of your tank. Never touch the plugs when your hands are wet. Always get an adult to handle the plugs for you.

The filter, heater, and air rock help keep your fish healthy by keeping their water just right.

Some tanks can sit on shelves, but most will need stands. Put a sheet of polystyrene under the tank. This stops the glass from breaking by spreading out the pressure on it.

At the bottom

You need to pick a **substrate**. This is the material that goes on the bottom of the tank. Medium to fine sand or gravel is best. It should be smooth, so your fish do not get hurt on it. Do not pick very coarse gravel. Dirt falls between the gaps and it is very hard to clean out. Darker colours will look the most natural.

Most people also get a background. It helps the fish to feel at home, and also looks nice. Most people stick a printed sheet on the outside of the tank. You can find moulded backgrounds that you glue to the inside of the tank before you add the water, but these can be hard to keep clean.

Choose your substrate, background, and decorations to make your fish feel at home. They also make the tank more interesting to look at.

Clean water

Even the best **filter** cannot keep the water completely clean. You need to replace some of the water every two weeks or so. Before you add new water, you should treat it with a **water conditioner**. It is a good idea to get a water testing kit. You might also like to get some chemicals for correcting the water if you ever need to. Ask your dealer what is best for the tap water where you live. You will need a tool called a siphon to move water in and out of the tank. The best ones have a bulb you squeeze to get the water moving.

Extras

You will need a few other things when you are ready to start. You will need one or two fine mesh green nets to catch your fish. An **algae** scraper is used to clean algae off the sides of the tank. Your fish depend on the filter, heater, and light to keep them healthy, so keep some spare parts in case anything breaks. Many people also have a hospital tank, to put sick fish in. A hospital tank can be a small plastic tank with a small filter and heater.

The chemicals, siphon and algae scraper all help keep the tank water clean.

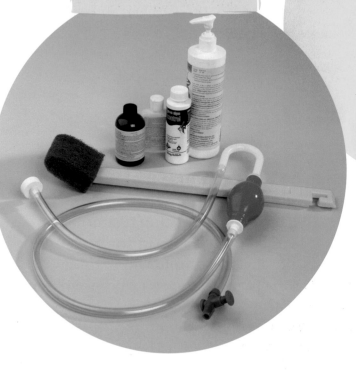

All tanks need a thermometer to tell you the water temperature. You can choose ones which go on the inside or outside of the tank.

Getting the water right

The water in your **aquarium** must be just right for your fish to live in. The fish you choose should all like the same type of water.

This aquarium is in perfect balance. The water is just right for the fish and plants that live in it.

Temperature and pH

The temperature needs to be within a range that is not too hot or too cold for your fish. The water must not be too **acidic** or **alkaline** for your fish. You measure this using a simple test called a "**pH** test". You take a small amount of the water and add a drop of testing liquid to it. The sample will change colour. You then compare the colour to a chart and it will tell you the pH of the sample. If it is too acidic or alkaline, you can use a treatment kit to correct it. After you treat it, you will need to test another sample to make sure it is right.

Hardness

Water can be "hard" or "soft". Water **hardness** refers to how many minerals are dissolved in the water. Some fish like hard water and others like soft water. You can test water hardness in the same way as you test for pH, using a special kit. You can treat it in the same way too.

Tap water contains chemicals that are bad for all fish. One, called **chlorine**, is a gas which usually goes into the air over a couple of days. But to be sure, it is still a good idea to treat your tap water for it. Others, such as **fluoride**, always need treatments to get rid of them. Ask your fish supply shop what your tap water will need to be treated for.

Top tip

Your tap water may have other chemicals in it that are bad for fish. They may be impossible to get out. You may need to use special water without any minerals to keep your fish in. Ask your pet store for advice.

Testing kits are easy to use and do not cost much. Ask your fish supply shop how often to use the ones they recommend. There are special kits for new tanks.

Nitrogen balance

The water is not the only thing that must be balanced properly for your fish. There is a cycle in nature that filters the waste out of water and makes it healthy for animals and plants to live in. It is called the **nitrogen cycle**. In an aquarium, the **filter** keeps this cycle going. It also picks up large bits of waste floating in the water.

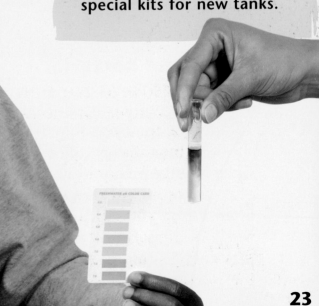

The nitrogen cycle

The **nitrogen cycle** is a process that will happen in your tank. The cycle starts when **bacteria** break down the waste that fish make. The waste turns into harmful **ammonia**. Then more bacteria turn the ammonia into **nitrites**, which are also harmful. Finally, another kind of bacteria turns the nitrites into **nitrates**, which are harmless. Nitrates even feed live plants. Live plants help the cycle work well, but they are not necessary. Over time, even with plants eating some of the nitrates, the nitrates build up in the tank water. When you change some of the water every two weeks, enough nitrates are removed to keep the water healthy.

The nitrogen cycle keeps all the food and waste in the water in balance.

Filters and bacteria

In order for this cycle to work, the sponge in the **filter** needs to have a good **colony** of the right bacteria. It takes about 36 days for the cycle to get working in a new set-up. You can shorten this time by adding gravel from an existing tank, since it will already have the right bacteria in it. You can also get treatment drops to add the bacteria to your new filter. When you clean out your filter, just swish out the solid waste in a bucket of tank water. You do not want to rinse out the bacteria colony you worked so hard to get going!

Keep it going

For the cycle to keep working well, you need to make sure there is enough **oxygen** in the water. Fish also need oxygen to breathe. Oxygen is given off in small amounts by live plants. Most of it comes from the air above the tank. **Air rocks** (see page 18) help move the water, making ripples that let more oxygen enter the tank.

You can see that this tank is out of balance! But often you cannot see that there is a problem because dangerous chemicals, such as ammonia and nitrites, are invisible.

Balance

- A healthy **aquarium** is in balance. It will be the best place for your fish to live.
- When an aquarium is out of balance, the water may smell or go cloudy. The fish or plants may get sick or even die.
- If the water seems off balance but your tests are all coming out fine, talk with your fish supply shop for more ideas.

Air rocks are easy, pretty ways to get more oxygen into the tank.

Setting up your tank

Now you are ready to set up your new **aquarium**. Before you begin, make sure you have an adult to help with the heavy lifting. Water may be clear and look light, but it weighs a great deal!

Work safely

You must also have an adult to help you with electrical items. Water and electricity do not mix. Even though all electrical items made for use with fish are safe around water, the plug and wall socket must be well away from water. When you plan how the cables and plugs will reach the sockets, make sure no-one can trip over them. Make sure the cables are safely and neatly tidied out of the way.

Planning ahead

Remember to plan ahead! Leave about a week between setting up the tank and adding one or two hardy fish. The **ammonia** from these fish will start the **nitrogen cycle**. You can also buy some products that speed up the cycle, but it usually takes about a month, and must be complete before you add any sensitive fish.

Step-by-step

1. Wash out the new tank, but never use any soap on anything for fish. Mix a little salt into tap water and use that to wash with. Rinse the salty water off with tap water.

2. Set the stand up where it will be staying. Put a polystyrene sheet on the stand (see page 19). Put the tank on the polystyrene.
3. Glue the background onto the outside of the tank and give it time to dry. A background helps fish to feel safe, since it gives them somewhere to hide.
4. Wash the **substrate** in running water until it is clear of any dirt. When you put it into the tank, rake it up so the back is higher than the front.

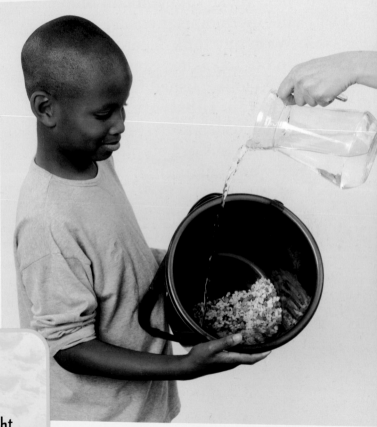

Top tip
Did you know that fish, like most living creatures, need day and night to stay healthy? Most like twelve hours of light and twelve hours of darkness. You may need a timer on your tank's light so it switches on and off automatically.

Getting ready for water

1. Read the instructions for your **filter**. Put the pipes and filter box in their places. Connect them all up.

2. If you are using a heater, read the instructions for it. Put the heater in the correct place. Also, place your thermometer where the instructions say it will work best. Make sure you can read the thermometer easily!

3. Wash any tank decorations in hot tap water. Some may need to be pushed firmly into your **substrate**. Add any plastic plants. Set up the decorations as you planned in your tank plan.

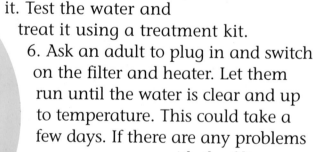

4. Now you can add the water. You can use water straight from the tap, but make sure it hits a rock or something large as it falls into the tank. If it goes straight onto the substrate it will make a hole in it.

There are many types of filter. Ask your local fish store which one they recommend for your tank.

5. When the tank is about two-thirds full, stop filling it. Test the water and treat it using a treatment kit.

6. Ask an adult to plug in and switch on the filter and heater. Let them run until the water is clear and up to temperature. This could take a few days. If there are any problems with the filter or heater, you can get them fixed before you put any fish in the tank.

Ask an adult to help you set up your tank.

Planting

There are many live plants you can choose for your **aquarium**. Some come with roots, to plant into the substrate. Some float on the surface of the water. Some come as **cuttings**, which then grow their own roots over time. Ask your dealer which ones will be best for your fish. Live plants help the water cycle and feed some fish. But they can be very hard to keep alive, so do not feel too bad if yours do not do well. Try different types, or switch to plastic plants.

Java Fern

Green Cabomba

Java Moss

Some plants are easier to keep than others. Ask your fish store for advice.

29

Adding plants

When the water is clearer and has reached the temperature it should be, you can add your plants.

1. Look at your tank plan as you work. Start at the back with the tallest plants and plant them in the **substrate**.
2. Finish with the shortest plants at the front and the floating ones in the water.
3. When you are happy with the planting, top up the water with tap water. Pour gently, so your planting is not ruined.
4. Fit the **hood** to the tank. Follow the instructions carefully. Ask an adult to plug in the light and set the light's on-off timer if you are using one. Always unplug the light before you take the hood off.
5. Turn on the **filter**, heater, and light. If you see any big bits of rubbish or dead plant material, take them out.

Adding fish

After a few more days, add a few hardy fish to start the **nitrogen cycle**. Ask your pet shop which fish are good. Test your water regularly, and when the cycle is complete, you can add more fish. Add one type of fish at a time, and leave about a week between each type. It may feel like it is taking a long time, but it will be fun to watch as your **aquarium** changes and grows.

If you do not put the tall plants at the back and the short plants at the front, you may never see your fish!

30

Water temperature

When you get your fish home from the dealer, do not open the bag straight into your tank. The new fish need to get used to the water temperature first. Float the clear plastic bag in your tank without opening it up. After about 30 minutes, you can let the fish swim out into their new home. Some experts say you should not let the water from the bag get into your tank. This is hard to do without hurting the fish. Try to get as little water as possible into your tank, but do not worry too much.

After floating the bag for about 20 minutes, add some tank water to the bag. Wait for five minutes and repeat. Then let your fish swim into their new home.

Feeding your fish

When you are planning your tank, talk to your fish dealer to make sure the fish you choose will be easy to feed. Some fish are fussy, or it is difficult to get the right type of food for them. Most fish that are good for beginners will eat dry food. Dry food is the most common kind of fish food. It comes as flakes, tablets, or pellets you buy from a fish supply shop. The flakes float on the top and feed the surface- and middle-swimming fish. Tablets sink to the bottom and feed the bottom-swimming fish.

Dry fish food comes in different forms. It has most of what fish need to eat in it.

bloodworm

daphnia

tubifex

Live and frozen foods give fish variety, fibre, and different **nutrients**.

brine shrimp

Live and frozen food

All fish like a little variety in their diet. About once a week, it is good to feed something different. They will welcome live and frozen foods. Brine shrimp, daphnia, tubifex, and bloodworms are good options. All of these are tiny animals that fish eat in the wild. You can add lettuce leaves pushed into the **substrate** and fresh or frozen peas squashed slightly as treats for your fish as well. Take the lettuce and peas out if they are not eaten after a few hours.

When to feed?

Many experts recommend that you feed your fish dry food every other day to start with. It is important that no wasted food is left to **pollute** the water. Your fish should eat all their food in about two minutes. If they do, you can try feeding more often. Some fish need feeding twice a day, others are fine once every two days. Experiment until you get the right amount for your fish. When you have a routine, make sure you stick to it. Fish like a regular schedule. Different feeding times each day will make them **stressed**.

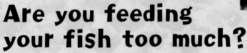

Your fish should eat in a hurry and finish all their food in about two minutes.

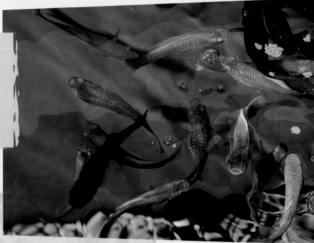

Are you feeding your fish too much?

- If there is food left over after two minutes, you need to clean it out. Give less food next time. Leaving food in the tank will make the water unhealthy. There may be fuzz or clumps of old food left on the bottom, too.

- If your fish are getting fat, they are eating too much. Some fish grow quickly, but they should grow evenly. If their stomachs are swelling but the rest is staying the same size, they could be overfed. If only one fish looks this way, it could be pregnant. If you are not sure, ask your fish dealer.

33

Keeping the tank clean

Keeping a healthy tank is the best way to keep healthy fish. The **aquarium** is much more crowded than a natural wild **habitat**. It needs your care to keep it healthy and in balance.

Every day

- Check the fish are healthy.
- Check that the water temperature is correct.
- Check that all the equipment is working.
- Feed your fish (some fish need feeding every two days).

Every week

- Clean the **hood** – but make sure you get an adult to unplug it first.
- Top up the water in your tank. Use tap water you have treated already. Remember to add the new water gently.
- Clean **algae** off the sides of the tank with a scraper.

When you clean off the algae, make sure you leave a little for the fish that like to eat it.

Every three weeks

- Stir the top of the **substrate** and siphon out any dirt.
- Do a partial water change.
- Check plants, remove any dead leaves, and trim them back if you need to. Some plants grow very quickly and can try to take over.
- Use your testing kit to check the water **pH**, **hardness**, and anything else your dealer recommends. Use your treatment kit if you need to correct anything.
- Check the **filter** sponge or material. If it is full of solid waste, take it out and wash it in the bucket of old tank water. Do not rinse it under a running tap because this will wash away the good **bacteria colony**.

Water changes

- To do a water change, prepare new water first. Treat the tap water and leave it for a few days in a bucket.
- Make sure the new water is close to the tank water temperature. Add a little hot water if you need to raise the temperature. Water that is too cold will **stress** your fish and plants.
- Use a siphon to clean the substrate as you remove the water. Take out about a tenth of the water. Do not take out any fish! Add the new water gently.

To siphon out old water, put a bucket below the tank level. Start the siphon and remove dirt from the substrate as well as water.

Every two months

- Change the **filter** material if needed. Never change all of it since that would take out the whole **bacteria colony**.
- Check the filter, heater, and other equipment. Ask an adult if you need to service the equipment or replace any parts. Your fish depend on the filter and heater to keep their tank healthy. If they stop working for more than a few hours, it could be serious. You should always have spare parts ready.
- Clean the filter pipework using hot water. Do not use any kind of soap.

Every six months

- Check the lighting tubes and get an adult to replace them if needed. You should have spare lighting tubes in case one burns out unexpectedly.

Cleaning the filter can be messy, but it is a very important job.

Set aside a special pair of scissors to use for trimming your **aquarium** plants.

Safety first

Always remember that water and electricity do not mix.

- Never put your hands in the tank water when any of the equipment is plugged in.
- Ask an adult to make the tank safe by unplugging the filter, heater, and light.

Changing the lighting tubes can be difficult. Ask an adult to do this for you.

Top tip

Looking after the everyday needs of your fish is fairly easy. But the weekly and monthly things can be harder to remember.

- Try making a list or chart to tell you what needs to be done and when.
- Or you could mark a calendar if that works better for you. Leave your reminder list near the tank, so you can see it easily.

37

Common problems

The water in your tank always has tiny **bacteria**, **fungus**, and **parasites** in it. Healthy fish are not affected by these things. But if the tank gets out of balance, the fish get weak and they can take over. Keeping the tank healthy is the best way to keep the fish healthy, too.

A healthy aquarium

Even the most careful fish owner will sometimes have problems. You can keep spare parts for your **filter**, heater, and lighting so they can be fixed quickly. What if your house suffers a power cut? First, do not panic. Most power cuts are over fairly quickly. If yours goes on for over a day, there are some things you can do. Every day, change about a tenth of the tank's water. Check the temperature, and if possible, add heated water if the temperature has fallen. Do not overfeed!

Fin rot makes fish look ragged. It is caused by bacteria.

Other problems

- If your **aquarium** starts to leak, you may be able to seal it up with silicone (waterproof sticky goo) from the fish supply shop. Ask your local dealer for advice.
- Tell family and visitors not to tap the tank. Tapping the glass sounds very loud to the fish and makes them **stressed**.
- Do not put plants you find in rivers or ponds into your tank. They may have parasites living in them which could unbalance the tank. If you see a snail living in your tank, take it to the fish shop and ask what you should do.

A sick fish?

Watching your fish will help you learn their usual behaviour. Look out for fish that are behaving in a new way. Hanging near the surface or bottom, staying very still, or holding their fins in can mean a fish is ill. Some diseases are easy to see, such as if the fish is covered in spots, fluff, or worms.

Top tip

To catch a fish, gently put one net into the water. Use another net to guide the fish into the first net. Always move slowly. When you have finished with your nets, clean them in warm water or in a special chemical you can buy from the fish supply shop.

This fluffy stuff is a fungus that has grown where the fish's body was hurt.

Green nets are a good idea. Fish may think they are plants and swim into them for safety.

Hospital tank

It is a good idea to have a hospital tank set up in case one of your fish gets seriously ill. It does not need much in it. To keep it healthy, it needs a little **substrate** and a smaller **filter** and heater than your main tank. Adding a few plastic plants will help make the fish feel safe. If you have to move a sick fish to the hospital tank, keep an eye on your other fish in the main tank in case they become ill, too.

If your fish is really sick, it may need to be kept alone in a hospital tank.

Treatments

To treat most illnesses, you add medicine to the water in the tank. It is very important that you treat the water for as long as it says on the medicine packet. Even if the fish look well again sooner, finish the treatment or your fish will get infected again. Stick with one treatment until its full cycle is over. If it has not worked, then try a new one. Switching treatments too soon can make the fish get sicker.

There are not many vets who treat fish, so it is a good idea to ask an expert from a fish supply shop or fish club about puzzling illnesses. Most treatments are for the water in your tank. You get them from fish supply shops.

Common diseases

- **Fungus** – this looks like cotton wool stuck on the fish (see picture on page 39). You can treat it with a salt bath (see Top Tip) or medicine that goes in the tank water.
- Fin rot – fin rot gives a fish ragged or rotted fins (see page 38). Again, try a salt bath or medicine in the tank water.
- White spot or Ich – white spots that look like grains of sugar appear on the fish's body. It is caused by **parasites** and is treated by adding medicine from the fish supply shop to the tank water.

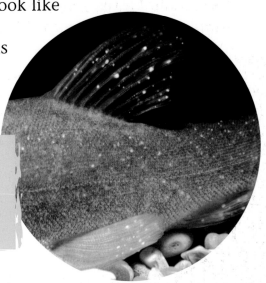

White spot, or Ich, spreads very quickly through the whole tank. Treat the main tank water.

Top tip

- To make a salt bath for sick fish, use a clean bowl or very small tank. Add a teaspoon of **aquarium** salt to each litre (quart) of water.
- Put the fish in the bath for about 15 minutes, but take it out if the fish seems unhappy. You might need to use less salt.
- Use a salt bath once a day until the disease has gone. Some fish are very sensitive to salt, so ask an expert before you treat a fish.

A salt bath may cure fungus or fin rot.

Parasites

Parasites are small creatures, such as worms or mites, that live on or in another creature. They can cause all sorts of problems. As well as white spot, different parasites can cause swollen eyes and holes in fish's heads. Slimy or velvety patches on the fish are signs of parasites. Parasite worms inside and outside the fish's body are also problems. If your fish have any of these problems, talk to an expert. Treatment depends on what kind of parasite it is and how sick the fish is.

A bowl is not a good home for fish! There is not enough oxygen and it is too small.

Other problems

Fish can become starved of **oxygen** if there is not enough getting into their water. They will stay gasping at the surface to try and get more. Do a partial water change as an emergency measure. Then think of how to get more oxygen into the water. An **air rock** can help by moving the water.

All aquariums have some **algae**, and some fish like to eat it. Too much may mean your tank is out of balance. Check the water **pH** and **hardness**, correct it, and clean off the algae. If the water is fine, maybe the light is on for too long each day.

Fish can get constipated, which means their **digestive systems** are not working well. They cannot push their food through properly. If any of your fish have very bloated stomachs or **faeces** hanging from their vents, they are constipated. Feed them more green vegetables such as lettuce and peas (see page 32). Also, try giving them live or frozen food such as brine shrimp.

This tank has far too much algae. It needs to be cleaned and the water needs to be tested.

Saying goodbye

Different fish live for different lengths of time. Even with the best care, some of your pet fish will die of old age or disease.

- If you find one floating in the **aquarium**, take it out with a net. It may be a shock to you, but do not blame yourself. There was probably nothing else you could have done to help it live longer.
- It is normal to feel upset when a pet dies. It may help you to have a special burial place for your fish.

Keeping a record

It is fun to watch your fish in their **aquarium**. Keeping a scrapbook lets you record that fun and remember it later. You can make notes about your fish's routines, what they eat, and how you care for them.

Even before you start setting up your tank, use a scrapbook to write down what you are learning. As you choose what to put in your tank, draw your tank plan in your scrapbook. Make notes about what choices you have made and why you have made them. If there are different ways to set up your tank, such as other plants or fish you could try, make notes about that, too. You may need to make changes later on, and your notes could help you to try new ideas.

Whenever you add new fish or plants, write about the ways you handled the changes. How did the new creatures like their home? What would you try differently next time?

Notes and photos

It is a good idea to include photos in your scrapbook. Show the tank at all stages of setting it up. As you add fish, take new pictures. You can write about why you chose those fish, and how you felt when you brought them home. If you visit a big aquarium, write about what you saw.

Your notes can help when things go wrong. If any of your fish get ill, take pictures and make notes about what you saw and did. If you need to ask an expert for advice, or if a similar problem happens again, your scrapbook will help you remember the details. Keep the numbers for your fish dealer and vet, if you have one, in your scrapbook.

After you put photos in your scrapbook, make sure you add labels to say what they show!

Top tip

Fish-keepers' clubs are good places to talk about problems and successes. Ask at your school and at your fish dealer if they know of any. If not, you could start your own. You can also ask an adult to help you find a discussion board on the Internet if you need advice. Many pet shop sites or sites about special types of fish have discussion boards.

These children meet once a month to talk about the fish they keep.

Glossary

acidic   sour kind of liquid

adapted   changed to suit a new environment

air rock   small rock with holes connected to a pump. Sends air bubbles into the water

algae   tiny water plants that grow together to make a furry coating

alkaline   liquid made of special salts mixed into water

allergic   when a person or an animal reacts badly to something they eat, breathe, or are stung by

ammonia   a chemical that is given off when plants and animals break down after they have died

aquarium   tank usually made of glass or plastic with see-through sides

bacteria   tiny one-celled creatures that can cause disease or help in breaking down plant or animal matter

breed   when animals mate to have babies

chlorine   a chemical found in most tap water, and swimming pool water

cold-blooded   animal having the same body temperature as the surrounding air or water

colony   group of creatures that live together

cool box   special container that keeps the temperature even inside

cuttings   bits of plants that can grow into new plants

digestive system   part of the body that changes food to energy and waste

environment   the kind of place something lives in, with its plants, animals, weather, temperature, and landscape

faeces   solid waste passed out of the body

filter   machine that helps to keep the water clean

fluoride   a chemical commonly added to water to help people's teeth stay strong

fry   baby fish that are born live instead of in eggs

fungus   a type of living thing such as mushrooms and mould

habitat   the environment where a plant or animal naturally lives

hardness   the measure of how many minerals are dissolved in water

hood   top that covers the tank

isolated   kept on its own

nitrates   the end product of the nitrogen cycle – nitrates are generally harmless chemicals that are used as food by plants

nitrites   chemicals made as the nitrogen cycle goes along. Nitrites are dangerous to fish and need to be turned into nitrates

nitrogen cycle   the cycle that turns waste products from plants and animals into food for plants

nutrients   the things in food that animals and plants need to stay healthy

oxygen   a gas in air and water that animals need to breathe in order to live

parasites   small creatures, such as worms or mites, that live on or in another creature

pH   measure of how acidic or alkaline a liquid is

pollute   to make dirty with rubbish or chemicals

school   a group of fish that swim together

stressed   made unhappy

substrate   the material put on the bottom of an aquarium

taste buds   things that people and animals use to taste their food

tropical   tropical fish live in water that is quite warm in areas near the equator

water conditioner   a special liquid that takes chlorine out of tap water

Further reading

Care for Your Tropical Fish, RSPCA Pet Guides Series (Collins, 2005)

Looking After Your Goldfish, Helen Piers (Frances Lincoln, 2002)

The Wild Side of Pet Fish, Jo Waters (Raintree, 2005)

Tropical Fish Complete Pet Owner's Manual, Peter Stadelmann and Lee Finley (Barron's Educational Series, 2003)

Useful addresses

Most countries have organizations and societies that work to protect animals from cruelty and to help people learn how to care for the pets they live with properly.

UK
Royal Society for the Prevention of
 Cruelty to Animals (RSPCA)
Wilberforce Way
Southwater
Horsham
West Sussex
RH13 9RS
Tel: 0870 33 35 999
Fax: 0870 75 30 284

Australia
RSPCA Australia Inc
PO Box 265
Deakin West ACT 2600
Australia
Tel: 02 6282 8300
Fax: 02 6282 8311

Internet
UK
RSPCA
www.rspca.org.uk

There's a special kids' section as well as general information, message boards and links to shops at www.fishkeeping.co.uk

General fish keeping information at fish.orbust.net and www.thetropicaltank.co.uk

Message boards and discussion forum at www.fishforums.net

Australia
RSPCA
www.rspca.org.au

Disclaimer
All the Internet addresses (URLs) given in this book were valid at the time of going to press. However, due to the dynamic nature of the Internet, some addresses may have changed, or sites may have changed or ceased to exist since publication. While the author and Publishers regret any inconvenience this may cause readers, no responsibility for any such changes can be accepted by either the author or the Publishers.

Index